1000 Best
Homebuying
Secrets

Michael Flynn

SOURCEBOOKS, INC.
NAPERVILLE, ILLINOIS

Published by Sourcebooks, Inc.
P.O. Box 4410, Naperville, Illinois 60567-4410
(630) 961-3900
Fax: (630) 961-2168
www.sourcebooks.com

Library of Congress Cataloging-in-Publication Data

Flynn, Michael
  1000 best homebuying secrets / Michael Flynn.
    p. cm.
  ISBN-13: 978-1-4022-0630-6
  ISBN-10: 1-4022-0630-5
  1. House buying--United States. 2. Residential real estate--Purchasing--
United States. I. Title: One thousand best homebuying secrets. II. Title.

HD255.F575 2005
643'.12--dc22

                                        2005025002

          Printed and bound in the United States of America.
              VP   10 9 8 7 6 5 4 3 2 1

To Fred & Stella, Ted & Josie...believers in the American Dream.

Contents

Acknowledgments ix
Introduction 1

One:
First Things First: Before You Begin 5
Are You Ready to Buy? 8
Creating a Wish List .13
Your Real Estate Agent 16
Choosing an Area 34
A Few Things to Keep in Mind
    While You Search .46
Know the Lingo 47
Know Your Rights 56

Two: Money Matters 59
Be Prepared 62
Finding a Mortgage Representative 64
How Much Can You Borrow? 65
Improving Your Credit 73
Preapproval: An Important Step 81
Wading through Your Lending Options 85
Tips for Taking a Mortgage 113
Mortgage Snafus 117

Know Your Rights 120
Taxes 124
More Key Players 132
Insurance 136

Three:
Finding the Right Type of Home for You 151
Condos and Co-ops: the Difference 154
New Construction 160
The Fixer-Upper 169
Is a FSBO Right for You? 185
Landmark or Historic Status 196

Four: Closing in on the One 201
House Hunter's Tool Kit:
    Things to Bring and Arrange 204
Timing Is Key 209
Seasonal Considerations 211
"Hot" Markets 213
When You Think You've Found It 222
Resale Factors 231

Five: Making the Offer
...and What Comes Next 237
The Offer 240
Getting Past the Co-op Board 251
After the Offer Is Accepted 254
Attorney Review 262
Home Inspection 268
Areas of Interest 275

Six: Tying Up Loose Ends 309
Repairs 312
The Walk-through 314

Seven: The Closing and Beyond 319
Escrow 322
The Closing 324
When Things Go Wrong .330

Glossary 339

Real Estate Acronyms 357

Internet Resources 358

Your To-Do List
during the Homebuying Process 359

Budget Plan 363

Wish List and House Hunting Log 367

Index 373

About the Author .385

Acknowledgments

Many people should be thanked for their valuable input into this book. Jacky Sach, my agent extraordinaire at BookEnds, made the process positive and exciting. Special thanks to Bethany Brown from Sourcebooks who made this book what it is, and of course to my fellow agents at Weichert Realtors in Basking Ridge, NJ, who make every experience a learning experience. Thank you to Joy Kenyon Venkor and Kelly Gordon for sharing their years of real estate insight.

No acknowledgment would be complete without thanks to my wife Jessica, whose enthusiasm and support make all things possible in my world.

Introduction

Whether you are looking at houses, condos, or co-ops, buying a home is one of the most exciting and nerve-racking experiences you'll ever have. For many of you, it's your biggest financial investment, and probably the most money you'll ever spend on one single purchase. It's also a lot more than simply finding the building of your dreams. Buying a home means making a determination about how and where you want to live. Do you want to live in the city, or do you dream of wide-open spaces, tall trees, and a backyard? Are you looking for a home to raise your family in, or something to just get you started—a simple one-bedroom? Do you look forward to spending weekends gardening, painting walls, or repairing the roof? Or do you want to keep your Saturdays free for fun?

As a licensed Realtor and homeowner, I understand the decisions homebuyers face, and know that whether it's your first home or fifth, buying a home can be a daunting and difficult task. My job is not only to find you the home of your dreams, but also to help you through the process. By writing this book, I'm hoping to put the power into your hands and make homebuying a simpler, more enjoyable task. Most importantly, I want to give you a thorough understanding of what to expect during each step of the process and how to prepare for any problems that might arise.

By putting together a simple list of one thousand tips, I have given you the knowledge you need to make the task easy, without bogging you down with information you don't need. Let's face it, most of us are busy, and buying a home only adds to your extensive list of things to do. Who has the time to wade through every detail of buying a home when all you really want to know is what's going to happen next and why? Because of that, I've prepared a book with quick tips and hints that can be skimmed, easily carried in your purse, pocket or glove compartment, and used at every stage of the experience.

In *1000 Best Homebuying Secrets* you'll learn how to prepare to buy a home before you even start looking, determine how much you can afford, and how and when to begin your search.

Within these pages, you'll find a wealth of key information on the following:

- Finding and working with a real estate agent and understanding what a realtor can do for you. (Did you know that for homebuyers, a realtor is free?!)
- Choosing a neighborhood or town that's right for you.
- The best times of day and times of the year to view a house.
- Choosing a mortgage.
- Making an offer and signing the contract.
- Understanding the home inspection process and the inspector's report.
- What to do when problems arise.
- Finding a lawyer and handling attorney review.
- Closing on your new home and moving in!

I hope you'll find this book a useful guide to your homebuying experience and, most importantly, I hope you find your experience more enjoyable because of the information you've received from me. As a realtor, I strive to make homebuying as painless as possible for my clients, and I hope that in these pages I'll do the same for you.

Happy hunting!
Michael Flynn

1.

First Things First:
Before You Begin

Looking for a new home is exciting; and it's only natural that once you've got the bug, you'll want to jump right in and start your search immediately. Before doing so, I suggest you read the following tips to get a better perspective on whether or not you are really ready to start looking for a home and, if you are, what kind of home you're looking for. You'll create a wish list so that you'll understand what you want; and if you are buying with someone else, you can make sure that both of you are on the same page. From there you'll get advice on choosing a neighborhood, reading real estate ads, and selecting an agent. You'll also learn those all-important terms of real estate that are bound to come up.

Are You Ready to Buy?

1. Are you looking to buy a home, an investment, or both? Your answer to this question determines the type of search you'll need. Finding the condo you want to rehab and sell in two years for a profit is very different from selecting the colonial on half an acre where you want to raise your children. Solidify in your mind what you are really searching for.

2. You may be able to afford more than you think. Many people's rental payments are approximately the same as their monthly mortgage payments would be. Current homeowners may have more equity in their homes than they realize, so don't count yourself out of a certain location or price range without doing your research first.

3. Before you buy, consider your current job potential. Are you waiting for a transfer? Are there rumors of a restructuring to come? Now may not be the right time to buy real estate.

4. Are you ready for the maintenance that a house, condo, or co-op requires? Even condos and co-ops with monthly fees still require at least some care and maintenance by the owner.

5. Consider the current status of your marriage or relationship. Ask yourself these tough questions: "Is now the time in our relationship to buy real estate?" "Is this the right person to be buying a house with?" Because of the costs and commitment, purchasing a house can put stress on even the strongest of relationships. Reselling the house will take time, even in a strong sellers' market, and there are many financial costs associated with it as well. Be sure you are ready.

6. People often ask, "When is the bubble going to burst on real estate?" Historically, home prices in the United States have not declined, primarily because homebuyers have treated their properties as homes rather than investments. Even homeowners whose homes have increased in value less than 1 percent per year have not panic sold because they consider their houses more than just an investment. In other sectors, true investors would generally sell off under-performing holdings.

7. Extremely hot markets where prices increase annually at rates of 10 percent or more tend to attract more investment buyers looking to make a profit, and this may drive the prices even higher. As with other investments, if the holding doesn't pay out to expectations (sometimes unrealistically high expectations), there may be a sudden glut of sellers. More sellers on the market typically flattens prices.

8. You may think you are being somewhat unreasonable when you consider moving because you cannot decorate or modify a rental the way you would like; but surprisingly, the limitations of living in a rental unit are one of the primary reasons people start their first house search. You have to get permission to make certain types of improvements, and does it make sense to spend thousand of dollars painting, carpeting, or tiling when it is the landlord who will benefit most from your work?

9. As a homeowner, you can make almost any changes you'd like, and you reap the benefits. Plus, you get to live in an environment you have created to suit your own tastes, not the specifications of some anonymous rental company.

10. Many buyers try to "wait out" a hot market. Unfortunately, no one can predict the future. Economic cycles, interest rates, and shifts in housing demand are virtually impossible to predict accurately. Plus, if you are both a buyer and a seller of real estate, there is no perfect market condition to do both simultaneously.

11. Don't think you can't, or shouldn't, buy a house, condo, or co-op because you aren't married or don't fit the "traditional" picture of a homeowner. According to the National Association of Home Builders (NAHB), married couples with children made up 50 percent of new homebuyers in 1985 but only 33 percent in 2001. In the same period, the percentage of single people buying new homes doubled to 14 percent in 2001 from 7 percent in 1985. Adult roommates, same-sex couples, married couples without children, and singles have become a force in the homebuying market.

12. You don't have to think of a house purchase as a lifetime commitment. You can sell the home in just a few years and ideally will have built some equity along the way. Career changes and new educational opportunities do not need to be impeded by home ownership.

Creating a Wish List

13. Create a wish list of what you are looking for in a house, condo, or co-op. Try to rank items by importance and consider which ones you would be willing to forgo if the right property was missing just one or two of them. Categorize items by "must have," "would like," and "in my dream world."

14. Wish lists are not just about bedroom count, bathroom size, and granite countertops. Remember to include important criteria such as location, overall size, and condition of the house as well as other important considerations like if high speed internet access is available in the area or, if you entertain regularly, whether the house can accommodate your guests.

15. If you are buying a home with your partner, a great exercise is creating individual wish lists. It's a great learning exercise to see what ranks at the top of your partner's list and to get her reaction to your list. Better to fight now than in the middle of an open house!

16. If an item from your wish list is not included in a specific house, consider the cost of adding it to the house later. Central air-conditioning may be quite easy to add to the house, but a fireplace may not be. Call a local contractor for an expert opinion and estimate.

17. If you are considering a fixer-upper, make sure you are clear with your agent about exactly what you consider doable. You may consider a fixer-upper a home needing a paint job and a new sink. Your agent may think you are looking for a row house with a missing roof, cracked windows, and a broken furnace.

18. It may be a big surprise, but it's not just first-time homebuyers who end up compromising on their wish list. Virtually all segments of buyers have to forgo some item on their wish list because of budget, availability, or timing.

19. Share your wish list with your realtor and elaborate on why certain items are on the list. Is that finished basement you want just a play area for your kids? The house that has an unfinished basement may work for you if it happens to have a large sunroom that could also work as a playroom. The more your agent understands your needs, the better he can help you.

20. Update your list as you see various homes. A week or two of searching may be a reality check—your "must haves" may not fit your price range, or you may find out that some of your "must haves" are not so important to you after you see a few properties without them. Scale back accordingly and keep your agent in the loop!

21. Well-meaning relatives, friends, real estate agents, or mortgage reps may encourage you to "overbuy," saying that although your mortgage payments may be financially pressing now, in a few years those same payments will be a smaller portion of your increased paycheck. You'll need to figure out what level of financial pressure you are willing to undertake. You can choose to "underbuy" or live below your means in anticipation of layoffs, child-rearing costs, or even saving for your next house.

Your Real Estate Agent

Why Work with a Real Estate Agent?

22. If you had $260,000 to invest in the stock market, you would probably seek out a financial planner to guide you through the process. According to figures released by the Federal Housing Finance Board, the average sale price of a single-family house in the U.S. was over $260,000! You'll want to spend wisely.

23. Are a real estate agent and a realtor the same thing? For the most part, yes. Both are licensed to buy and sell homes. "Realtor" is a registered trademark term for members of the National Association of Realtors, a private trade organization.

24. Do you know realtors work for free?! Well, not really, but they are generally free to homebuyers. Sellers usually pay the commission to their listing realtor as well as your realtor, so there is no out-of-pocket cost to you.

25. Make sure that your agent is licensed to buy and sell real estate in your state. Licenses are typically posted in the agent's office.

26. What are all those letters on your agent's business card? There are many specialties that real estate agents can take continuing education courses for, ranging from senior housing to second home purchasing. If you have a special housing need, it may be worth asking about.

27. Are brokers and agents the same thing? Brokers have continued their formal real estate training beyond the level required to become an agent and have passed a broker's exam. Becoming a broker usually allows individuals to open their own real estate agency. Agents have completed their state training and exam requirements and usually must work for a broker.

28. The difference between brokers and agents isn't very important for buyers and sellers. A broker has more technical training under his belt, but the important thing to buyers is that the broker or agent is out in the field helping customers each day. It is the neighborhood knowledge and understanding of the buying process that is going to be the most beneficial to you.

29. The agent's initial job is to find houses that match your wish list and budget. While you may feel that various Internet sites have all the information you need, agents will make it their daily responsibility to search the Multiple Listing Service (MLS) for housing coming on the market or changing in price. Websites available to the public sometimes have information that is several days old —not the kind of lag a buyer needs when the market is competitive!

30. Once you share the list of what you are looking for and fine tune it during the search, a realtor will weed out the houses that aren't even worth a "drive-by," saving you time after work, during lunch, or on weekends.

31. Even the newest agents know nuances of their local market: how much a house has recently sold for, how long a house has been on the market, and the details of recent bidding wars. All of this information can help guide you during your search and negotiating process. You'll want to know what current market conditions dictate so you can make your decisions with as much information as possible.

32. If you get to the negotiation stages, and a real estate agent sees things turning confrontational, she may be able to keep the deal afloat by playing down the emotions involved in the deal.

33. Most real estate agents have handled many deals in the past and will recognize problems before they arise. This could save you time, money, aggravation, and potentially, the deal.

34. Although you should always check with an attorney for legal advice, realtors can help explain the impact of legal points on your transaction.

How to Find a Real Estate Agent

35. Onc of the most useful tools in looking for a house is a real estate agent. The best way to find one is the old-fashioned way—word of mouth! Ask your neighbors, coworkers, friends, or even your doctor if she bought or sold a house recently, and if she was happy with her real estate agent. If she was, that person might work well for you too.

36. Attend open houses in the neighborhoods you are interested in. Chat with the agent who is working the open house. Ask questions about the house, the neighborhood, or whatever else you are interested in. If he is knowledgeable, and you think your personalities will work well together, he might be the agent for you!

37. Did an agent help you find your current home or apartment? Did you like working with her? Find out if she also helps homebuyers in the area you are considering.

38. Ask your realtor how many listings or sales they have had in the specific town, neighborhood, or condo community you are most interested in. You'll want an agent who is familiar with the prices there so she can help you make a better-informed decision.

39. Surf the Web. Sites such as realtor.com are great places to search for an agent. Search for agents working in the area you plan to buy and read each agent's profile and philosophy. See if it matches your personality and priorities.

40. Real estate companies usually have websites too. Go to such sites as weichert.com, coldwellbanker.com, etc., or find one for a broker in your area. Most sites have ways to search for agents. Be sure to read any information they've included about their work style and business philosophy.

41. Feel free to call or email an agent. As part of the selection process, most agents are happy to answer your questions or concerns. Agents who are too busy to reply may be too busy to work with you. Agents who do reply may have answers that match what you are looking for in a realtor. Realtor websites are full of email addresses and phone numbers for realtors, so contacting several should not be too difficult.

42. If you are in a rush, call a local real estate office and ask for the manager. Talk to her about your needs, your timing, etc. Based on your needs, she can connect you with an agent who may be a perfect fit. All it takes is a ten-minute conversation.

43. Hang on to any real estate mailings you get in the mail that you think provide useful information. If the realtor's mailings seem to meet your needs, he may be a good match for you when it comes time to buy your new home.

44. If you are interested in a specific neighborhood, condo community, or building, see if that community has its own newsletter. There may be a realtor ad for an agent who specializes in that area or even lives there.

45. Read the local newspaper. Look for houses that are for sale in the neighborhoods and price range that you are most interested in. The listings will usually include the agent's name and phone number. Give her a call!

46. Ask the security guard or the front desk clerk of the building if he knows an agent who sells frequently. That agent may be a perfect resource for you.

47. Places like community pools, libraries, and coffee shops are great places to strike up a conversation with the locals. Ask them if they know a good local realtor—almost everyone does.

48. Some realtors specialize in working with buyers, others with sellers; some are comfortable working with both. If you meet a realtor that only works with sellers, feel free to ask if he can recommend a buyer's agent.

49. Many realtors work in teams; so ask ahead of time to meet both people. You'll want to make sure you think both partners are agents whom you would like to work with.

50. Some busier agents have assistants who take care of the details after your offer is accepted. Ask your agent if he will be taking care of all of the details prior to closing. You should know ahead of time if your agent is simply getting you to the offer and the acceptance and his assistant is getting you to the closing.

51. If you think you will be more comfortable with a realtor who speaks a second language, consider looking in non-English newspapers, chat rooms, or message boards. Bilingual agents are sometimes noted on broker websites, or referenced on their own personal websites.

52. An agent in your current area may be able to refer you to an agent elsewhere in the region or country. Share your wish list with the referring agent to help her pick an appropriate agent for you.

53. Ask a prospective agent how proficient they are at emailing. You'll be surprised by the number of agents who are not comfortable emailing listings. If email is your primary mode of communication, make sure your agent is adept at it!

54. The quick and easy way to find an agent is to call or walk into a local real estate office. Usually the person answering the phone or sitting at the front desk is working what is called "opportunity time." That agent is just waiting for a new customer!

Who's Working for You? Buyer's Agents and Seller's Agents

55. Most states require that agents disclose their relationship as a seller agent or a buyer agent. A good agent will explain this the first time you meet, even without a law, but make sure you ask whom the agent is representing.

56. The commission paid by the seller for selling a house is agreed to prior to listing the property, usually somewhere between 5 and 7 percent. If a buyer's agent negotiates a deal on your behalf, the seller's agent splits the commission. If you buy without using a buyer's agent, the seller's agent, in many instances, keeps the full commission minus the real estate company's portion.

57. Buyers may think that if they don't have an agent, the seller should be able to negotiate for a lower commission and pass some of the savings along to the buyer. This rarely happens since the commission has already been agreed upon prior to listing the home.

58. Different areas have different forms of agent representation; ask what forms of representation are available in your area. Most states require that agents provide you with the details of representation in writing, so ask for a copy.

59. Buyer's brokers represent buyers, and it is their fiduciary responsibility to work in the best interest of the buyer throughout the process and to negotiate the best possible price and terms for the buyer. Information shared by the buyer with the buyer's broker is to be kept confidential unless it is expressly indicated that specific information be shared.

60. Seller's brokers represent sellers and that broker's fiduciary responsibility is to negotiate the best possible price and terms for the seller. Any information shared by the seller with the seller's broker is to be kept confidential unless it is expressly indicated that specific information be shared.

61. Disclosed dual agency exists when one real estate brokerage, not necessarily the individual agent, represents both the seller and the buyer in a transaction. This relationship is perfectly legal in many states; it must be disclosed up front verbally and usually requires a signed agreement by all parties. Another name for disclosed dual agency is a transactional brokerage.

62. Make sure you have a complete understanding of which side your agent's fiduciary responsibility lies.

33. As with any form, never feel pressured to sign on the spot. Take the time to review all agency relationship forms. Your agent should be happy to explain them to you fully.

34. If your agent happens to be the listing agent of a house you want to make an offer on, double check all agency relationship agreements and talk to the branch manager before moving forward.

35. Your agent may be able to represent both you and the seller at the same time legally. If you are not comfortable with such a situation, consider asking the broker for another agent who can represent you in the purchase.

36. In many areas of the country, agents ask prospective buyers to sign an agreement—make sure you read it before you sign it. You'll want to make sure that you can walk away from that realtor if things don't work out well.

67. You may want to keep your financial information fairly private from your agent. If you have told your agent that you want to spend around $400,000, it's not necessary to tell him you can actually afford $600,000.

68. One risk of not sharing your top number with your agent is missing what could have been your perfect dream house priced at $525,000 because, though you can afford $600,000, you told your agent $400,000 tops.

69. Negotiation is part of a real estate agent's job; therefore, if you find a house you love, but don't want to pay the asking price, talk to your agent about the possibility of making a successful lower bid.

70. The total commission paid is generally between 5 percent and 7 percent of the final closing price. Approximately half goes to the selling brokerage company and the other half goes to the buying brokerage company. The individual agents usually receive about half of their company's share.

71. Don't worry about working with a realtor even when you are "just looking casually" or "not ready to look seriously". Most realtors are happy to work at whatever pace you want, from emailing you listings just once a month, to showing you ten houses per day. Just let them know up front, so they know exactly what pace you are expecting.

Tips for Working with Your Agent

72. Tell your real estate agent what form of communication you prefer—home email, work email, phone, etc. You know best what the easiest way to contact you is.

73. Be open to your agent showing you homes that don't quite meet all of your parameters; she may be showing you exactly what is in your price range, or an alternative neighborhood you hadn't considered. An open mind may help you find a revised dream home!

74. Don't be surprised if your realtor isn't showing you the perfect houses on your first few outings. There is a learning curve with each agent. It takes time for the agent to get to know your exact likes and dislikes.

75. After each house visit, remember to share the positive and negative aspects of the house with your agent. It's the best way for him to learn your preferences.

76. If you are attending open houses without your agent, make sure you sign in using his/her name. This will help ensure that he/she can represent you, should you decide to make an offer on that specific house.

77. If you are moving into a new area and are unsure of which towns and neighborhoods you might prefer, ask your realtor to spend a morning or afternoon driving you around to familiarize yourself with the area.

78. Ask your agent to print out listings in your price range for each town or neighborhood you'll be looking at so you can familiarize yourself with the prices within the area.

Choosing an Area

When it comes time to move, be it across town, across the state, or across the county, there are many questions you'll need to consider: where to move, which house to buy, how much to offer, and how to actually get the house you want for a fair price. The process can be intimidating, overwhelming, and emotional. Answering some of the following questions and adopting the following tips will help make the process a little less stressful.

79. Give thought to what areas of the country or what parts of your state or region will offer the greatest selection of jobs in your career path. Coal miners may not want to move to Hawaii in search of work, and surf instructors might have a tough time in Pittsburgh.

80. The cost of living may greatly impact what homes you can afford. A website such as houseandhome.msn.com/pickaplace/comparecities.aspx can give you a good idea of how affordable different regions of the country are. If you are downsizing, you may choose a less expensive part of the country where your housing dollars will go even further.

81. If you think your relocation is temporary, consider the costs of moving both now and on your next move. If you're moving to a less expensive area, remember that your next move may take you back to an expensive region. When considering your house budget, talk to your financial advisor for the best approach to ensure that you'll be able to afford that move in the future.

82. If climate is of great importance to you, make sure that the region you are considering meets your needs. Also keep in mind that weather can differ greatly not only regionally, but also within a metropolitan area; so plan to choose an area best suited for you. Will the city's hilly region be treacherous in winter? Is the area near the bay foggier than the rest of town? How much hotter is the valley in summer? Ask your realtor, check weather.com, and if possible, visit the area to help determine if it is right for you.

83. If your heart is set on a newly con-structed home or brand new neigh-borhood, consider freshly developed areas of the south and west. Expansion in these regions offers homebuyers many new developments to choose from.

84. Consider the ties to your family. You may want to consider an additional bedroom for frequent family visits, and your long-distance move may cost a lot in airline flights for visits each year. Would a more manageable move two hours away by car meet your needs better? Figure the extra bedrooms and travel costs (for you and your kids!) into your monthly budgets.

85. If certain sports or recreational activities are very important to you and your family, you should consider that when choosing a region. Ice hockey is very popular in Minnesota and Massachusetts, while high school football is a premiere attraction in Texas. On a local level, you should consider the section of the state, county, or metropolitan area that allows you the easiest access to the activities you and your family love. You may not be willing to make a two-hour drive to ski or fish every weekend.

86. Traffic patterns can vary within the same area. Certain roads or freeways are more congested on a daily basis than others. Check traffic reports on local television each workday to see if the area you are considering is more prone to traffic than you are willing to tolerate. Think about what your daily commute will be like.

87. Make sure that charming ski town, antique center, or quaint city neighborhood you've got your eye on is not too overrun with tourists on weekends or vacation periods for your taste. Your home near the beach may be ideal Monday through Thursday, but the beach bound traffic on Friday afternoons may make for one tough commute. Visit the area during peak visitor time and check for traffic, parking, and noise problems.

88. Non-job commutes can also become quite taxing. Consider the convenience of everyday life. Are the supermarkets, schools, and trains conveniently located? Is the waterfront view you fell in love with at the open house worth the extra time you'll spend reaching the things you'll need every day?

89. Are you more drawn to water views or pre-WWII housing? There may be certain sections of your area that have a greater concentration of houses that meet your specifications. Discuss this with your realtor and concentrate your search there first.

90. Look to see if there are toll roads or increased mass transit costs around your new area. These additional costs, or ideal savings, should be a part of your monthly budget.

91. Look at taxes on an aggregate level. Some states have high income taxes but low or no property taxes. Others have higher property taxes to compensate for lower income taxes. Do certain counties or towns in the area have higher property tax levels than others? You'll want to incorporate this into your decision-making.

92. When you're looking at various communities, purchase into a town that has a viable and stable economy. When you want to sell your home five, ten, or twenty years from now, you'll want to know that your community will still be a desirable place to live. The "Rotary Phone Capital of the U.S." may not be an economic boomtown in ten years.

93. Don't just consider the commuting time to the job you have now. You may change jobs while you're living in your new home, so consider a location that allows you to commute to other business centers too. If you plan now, you may be able to choose a town that allows you to easily commute to several likely job centers.

94. Does your job or your spouse's job require out-of-town travel? Look to see how convenient those frequent trips to and from the airport will be. There is nothing worse than a two-hour car ride through terrible traffic after a delayed flight. Try finding a town conveniently located near two airports so that your traveler has the option of different airports.

95. Unless you like solitude or don't mind a longer commute, try not to choose isolated peninsulas, islands, or more remote sections of metropolitan areas. If your job routinely requires regional car travel, you may want a more central location.

96. Use websites such as mapquest.com to estimate distances and travel times to important travel points such as your work place, the airport, the local school, etc.

97. Consider in which direction a metropolitan area is growing. If your commute from the rapidly-growing northern suburbs is twenty minutes today, that ride could double with all those new commuters.

98. Schools are a very important factor to consider—even if you don't have kids. When it comes to reselling, your potential buyers may factor the school system into their buying decision when looking at your house.

99. Contact the local school district and ask if children always attend the school closest to their home. When overcrowding exists within a system, districts reshuffle. Being new in town, your kids may not be attending the school across the street but rather the one across town. If you see any auxiliary trailers outside the neighborhood school, chances are there is an overcrowding problem.

100. Make an appointment during the school day to see the school. Meet with teachers, administrators, and guidance counselors. Visit the school at drop-off/pick-up time to talk to some of the parents and get their opinions of the schools, the teachers, and the activities. Parents will be pretty honest and will also add dimension to the facts and figures the school reports!

101. If you are considering public school for your kids, make sure you know where the border line for the free school bus is in town. If you are considering private school, look for a house that is convenient for drop off and pick up on the way to and from work.

102. Local schools may also have websites—a great place for finding general information on the school such as instructional time, classes offered, enrollment deadlines, and administration contacts.

103. If your budget is relatively low for the geographic area that you are looking in, consider a town or area with less impressive schools or one where just the high school is a concern—you will most likely get more house for the money. This approach works best if your kids are infants or in early elementary school since it allows you time to move before the schools impact your family.

104. Look at what a town offers its residents. Is there a town pool or lake, a community center with fitness facilities, a public golf course, or a skate park? These amenities can help make life more enjoyable for the whole family, and if the town offers free or subsidized access to facilities you would normally pay for, the money you save can be passed on to your mortgage or your monthly bottom line!

105. What facilities or activities are offered for children, teens, and seniors? If your family includes members of these groups, a great public library, a skate park, or a senior center may not only make those members' day-to-day life more enjoyable, it might be a great relief to you as well.

106. Certain towns have seasonal activities that you may be specifically interested in such as farmers' markets, free concerts in the park, or holiday and festival celebrations. Ask your realtor or check individual town websites for information.

107. Many towns have their own websites, which are great resources. Use them to discover what towns have to offer and even uncover some future issues or benefits of the town.

108. Look at the rate of development in the area or neighborhood you are considering. Will the benefits that drew you there be increasing or decreasing over the next five or ten years? Read local newspapers and magazines, attend local community meetings, and talk to area residents and your agent to see what concerns the current residents have. Try to find out whether your potential neighborhood is about to be the next hot thing or the next big dud.

109. To help get a better understanding of prices in various towns or neighborhoods, window-shop the local real estate offices; many post houses and prices in their front windows.

110. Many people have made a lot of money buying into a neighborhood early, or have saved a lot on their purchase price by buying before a neighborhood is "discovered." Conversely, many people have bought into neighborhoods that have never taken off.

A Few Things to Keep in Mind While You Search

111. The biggest rule to remember is everything is negotiable. Chances are you are spending hundreds of thousands of dollars in a real estate transaction including not just the dwelling, but also the mortgage, the title search, the survey, the home inspection, and the movers. It never hurts to ask for a reduced price.

112. In most of the country, brand new construction is more expensive than construction from just ten years ago. Remember this when setting your budget and creating your wish list.

113. The average American moves every five to seven years. Although you may originally plan to stay in your new home for a "long time," you may decide to move in three years for a new job or because of a change in your family status. Keep this in mind when you are looking at homes and matching them to your wish list.

114. If you are single, childless, and in your twenties or thirties, consider that you may not be single or childless much longer. Life has a funny way of changing when you least expect it. The one-bedroom condo you are considering now may not be the ideal home five years from now.

Know the Lingo

Decoding the Ads

(Note: See page 357 for common real estate acronyms.)

115. "As is" condition can mean two things: one, the unit or house needs anything from cosmetic work to major renovations, or two, the seller may not make or pay for any repairs prior to closing.

116. Phrases such as "needs TLC (tender loving care)" or "diamond in the rough" can mean the house needs things as minor as tearing out wallpaper or as major as replacing heating and cooling units.

117. "Builder's dream" and "handyman special" usually refer to a house that requires extensive cosmetic and structural work.

118. "Motivated seller" may be code for "price is negotiable."

119. "Present all offers" may also mean that the price is negotiable at this point.

120. Words like "cozy," "cute," or "cottage" may actually mean small.

121. A "partial view" could be a very small view at an odd angle of a lake, river, park, or other appealing outdoor amenity.

122. "New" should mean new. Oddly, "newer" usually means "a couple of years old."

123. "Walkable," depending on the agent's interpretation, could mean anywhere from around the corner to a mile or more away. "Near" may be even further. Always check for yourself.

124. Generally, if an ad does not mention updated kitchens or baths, the house doesn't have updated kitchens or baths.

125. Square footage should be the measurable living space, not the total area within the perimeter walls. Space inside the living room, kitchen, bedrooms, etc., should be included, but space physically taken up by interior walls, closets, utility rooms, and the like should not be included. Practices vary from region to region and from broker to broker, so don't be surprised if there is some square footage lost to these interpretations. Some regions don't publish square footage for that very reason.

126. Sometimes condominium model names and/or numbers are actually square footage. The Clifton X1960 may in fact have approximately 1,960 square feet.

Real Estate Terms

127. "Real estate" is the land and all man-made improvements (buildings, utilities, etc.) on that land.

128. Real estate rights generally include the surface of the earth and extend to the center of the earth via subsurface rights. These rights include any natural resource below the ground such as water, oil, or minerals. Air rights extend outwards from the surface of the earth into space.

129. Landowners can sell their subsurface and air rights. Always check when purchasing a property if these rights have been transferred to another party.

130. With many people desiring waterfront views, more development is occurring on land bordering the ocean, lakes, and rivers affected by tides. These areas are referred to as littoral. Property lines on littoral lands generally extend to the mean high tide line. States have differing definitions of the mean high tide line, so check with your attorney or state government officials to find out what it is in your prospective state.

131. Land bordered or crossed by streams or other waterways are referred to as riparian. Generally, if the border line of two properties is a stream or river, the property line runs down the middle of the stream or river. If over the course of time that river or stream changes course, the property line remains in its original position.

132. Easements are rights of one party to use the land of another party for a specific use. The gas company may have an easement through a property for a gas line. That easement is for a specific use—a gas line, not a runway or office. Talk to an attorney and local government officials for specific information on easements.

133. Easement appurtenant is an easement that grants rights to the owner of a neighboring property. The owner of a lakeside property may grant a right-of-way access to the lake's beach to an inland neighbor.

134. Easements may be terminated when the original purpose no longer exists; for instance, if the lake mentioned above is drained.

135. The owner on the receiving end of an easement may release the giving owner from the easement.

136. An encroachment is the illegal placement of a physical object on a property by a non-owner. A fence that extends five feet into a neighbor's yard is an encroachment.

137. Surveys or physical inspection of the property are intended to discover encroachments. To remedy an encroachment, discuss the issue with real estate attorneys or local government officials.

138. Fixtures are any articles that are permanently affixed to the land or building that is being sold. Fixtures include heating and cooling systems, kitchen cabinets, bathroom tubs, and sinks. Sheds, fences and landscaping are also considered fixtures.

139. Depending on where you live, movable items such as refrigerators and stoves are excluded from the sale. Always ask for a list of exclusions prior to making an offer so that you know exactly what is included and excluded in the sale.

140. Double check items that fall into that gray area of exclusions such as affixed lighting fixtures, draperies, blinds, drapery poles, window air conditioners, etc. In many places, these items are considered personal property, so they would be excluded from the sale. Always ask so that there are no surprises.

141. If the seller is removing light fixtures, especially hanging light fixtures in entry foyers and dining rooms, ask your realtor what the seller plans on leaving behind. Sellers in your area may be obligated to replace the light with an inexpensive fixture or merely cap the wires. It's good to know ahead of time—you don't want to be left in the dark!

142. If the seller plans to replace any fixtures with inexpensive versions prior to leaving, consider asking for a credit equal to what they planned on spending. If the seller planned on spending $35 to replace the dining room chandelier, ask the seller to just cap the fixture upon removal and credit you $35. You can use the $35 to help fund the light of your choice. You may have replaced the seller's replacement light anyway.

143. Remember to calculate the cost of purchasing replacements for exclusions.

144. Deed restrictions are stipulations on the property placed by private parties, not the government, and can be placed on an individual property or on an entire development.

145. The restriction is written into the deed that transfers with the property. The restriction is binding on all future owners unless otherwise stated.

146. If a deed restriction and a zoning rule (from the government) cover the same topic, the more restrictive rule is the enforced code.

147. Title VIII of the Civil Rights Act of 1968, commonly referred to as the Fair Housing Act, prohibits discrimination in the sale, rental, and financing of dwellings based on race, color, national origin, religion, sex, handicap (disability), and familial status (including children under the age of eighteen living with parents of legal custodians, pregnant women, and people securing custody of children under the age of eighteen). Many states have additional protected classes. Check with your state to see what groups are covered.

148. Title VI of the Civil Rights Act of 1964 prohibits discrimination on the basis of race, color, or national origin in programs and activities receiving federal financial assistance. Section 504 of the Rehabilitation Act of 1973 prohibits discrimination based on disability in any program or activity receiving federal financial assistance. These laws are meant to protect buyers from discrimination when buying and financing a home.

149. Even if you may be interested in living in an area that is populated by people of a specific ethnic background, religion, or race, because of anti-discrimination laws, your real estate agent will not be able to discuss such issues with you.

150. Steering is the directing of home-buyers either to or away from particular areas based on race, religion, and country of origin or any other protected class. The Federal Fair Housing Act strictly forbids steering.

151. If you feel that an agent has acted in a discriminatory manner, contact your state's attorney general office for information about filing a complaint.

2.

Money
Matters

Affordability is one of the biggest obstacles in buying a new home, and should be one of the first things you look into when beginning your research. If you don't know how much you can afford, you won't even know where to start; therefore, once your wish list is in place and you have an understanding of real estate in general, read this section to gain a better understanding of how to find out what you can afford.

There are three important first steps in the financial aspect of the homebuying process. First, know how much money you need to borrow and how likely you are to get it. Second, research the many mortgage and financing options and decide which works best for your needs. Based on the first two steps, focus on the lenders that have the loan vehicles you want and are the most likely to lend them to you. Once you know what you can afford, it will be easier for you to know what type of home to look for.

Be Prepared

152. A little preparation time up front may prevent a crazy scramble when you are putting an offer together. Before you even get in the car with a realtor or start your internet search in earnest, you should be collecting pertinent paperwork that you'll most likely need: copies of federal tax returns, recent W-9s, employment verification letters, and savings and investment statements. You'll need these documents in order for a mortgage representative to determine how much of a mortgage you may qualify for.

153. Most lenders do not allow gifts from family members to count toward a down payment. Your lender will most likely ask you for information on any large transfer into your account, so it is difficult to hide. If a family member is interested in assisting you with a financial gift, encourage them to do so at least six months before your search begins.

154. The IRS gift maximum is currently $11,000 from parent to child. Ask your tax preparer for more information or go to www.irs.gov.

155. If you are currently renting, make sure you don't sign a twelve-month lease when you want to move in six months. See if a month-to-month lease is available or if there is an escape clause allowing you to give a month or two notice.

156. If you already have a lease lasting past when you'd like to move, find out what the penalties are for breaking your lease. The penalties should be written in the lease you signed. If there are penalties and you do decide to break the lease, include those costs in your monthly budget for the duration of the penalty period.

157. Most people budget their money on a monthly basis. They usually know how much they earn each month and what their current rent or mortgage payment is. Break down all the costs of your potential mortgage, taxes, insurance, and association dues into a monthly number so that you truly understand the impact of the home purchase on your budget.

Finding a Mortgage Representative

158. Talk to your friends, neighbors, and coworkers. One may have recently worked with a mortgage representative that he/she would highly recommend.

159. As the financial industry has evolved over the past decade, more and more institutions are able to facilitate mortgages. Your bank, credit union, or investment company may be able to assist you. Many large real estate companies also own or have a partnership with a mortgage company. Talk to your agent about what her company offers.

160. The Internet is an endless source of mortgage lenders. Do your research. You'll want to make sure your lender is reputable and there are no hidden charges or delays.

161. Don't sign anything you haven't read! Don't lock yourself into any agreements before talking to at least two or three mortgage representatives.

How Much Can You Borrow?

162. Not all borrowers are created equal! Lenders will judge you on three main criteria: credit rating, the loan-to-value ratio, and your income.

163. The better your credit rating, the better the rate and terms you will receive from a lender. The higher your FICO score (Fair Isaac Company Score), the lower the interest rate you will be paying.

164. Although there are several ways to report credit, FICO is the primary measure in today's market. FICO is a formula that Fair Isaac developed.

165. FICO scores are based on five basic categories in descending level of importance: payment history, outstanding debt, credit history, pursuit of new credit, and types of credit used.

166. Approximately 35 percent of your total FICO score is based on your payment history! Payment history includes not only late payments to creditors but also any past judgments, bankruptcies, or accounts in collection.

167. Approximately 30 percent of your FICO score is based on how much credit you use each month. Outstanding debt is the number of outstanding balances held by a borrower, average balance held by the borrower, and ratio of total balances to total credit limits on credit cards.

168. Approximately 15 percent of your FICO score is based on credit history. Credit history is how long a borrower has established credit. Generally, a shorter history is riskier to a lender since the borrower hasn't proven her ability to pay all debts in a timely, consistent manner. If older credit cards or loans are no longer active, credit history may only include your oldest current form of credit.

169. FICO scores range from 375 to 900. The higher the FICO score, the better credit risk you are.

170. A FICO score of 660 or greater usually indicates a good credit risk.

171. A FICO score between 620 and 660 is an average credit risk.

172. FICO scores below 620 are generally considered riskier. Lenders may be willing to lend money to such a borrower at higher rates than they would charge to borrowers with higher FICO scores.

173. If your FICO score is low, the credit report will explain why.

174. A more recent loan is going to hurt your credit score more than an older loan. FICO looks at the ratio of the original loan amount to the outstanding balance. Chances are you owe a higher percentage of the original loan amount for your 2005 auto than your 1999 auto.

175. Some credit card companies report your actual credit limit. Some only report the highest balance you've ever charged on your card. If your current balance is $1,500 on a $5,000 credit limit, you should be fine. If that same balance of $1,500 is on a credit card where your company only reported your highest balance of $2,000, your credit rating could be reduced.

176. Even if you pay your credit cards completely each month and carry no balance month-to-month, your credit card company will most likely report a balance anyway. If a credit report is run on the 15th, and your bill is not due until the 30th, the credit card company will report that as a balance.

177. Pay your credit card balance more than a week prior to the monthly statement date; that is when most credit card companies report balances to credit bureaus.

178. Types of credit in use is a measure of the number of various forms of borrowing utilized by the borrower. Lenders like to see a record of consistent, timely payments in a variety of borrowing options so they know the borrower has a track record of managing different types of debt: credit cards, auto loan, mortgages, etc.

179. If you have never taken out a mortgage or never had an auto or student loan, but have made timely payments on two credit cards and kept the balances low, your credit history should be well rated.

180. Pursuit of new credit is a measure of how many inquiries and new accounts there have been made by or regarding a specific borrower. The more new accounts, or inquiries for new accounts, the riskier the borrower. Lenders feel that the borrower may be increasing their debt elsewhere.

181. Loan-to-value (LTV) ratio helps the lender determine how much money they will lend you. The usual limit is 80 percent of the appraised value of the home you are considering.

182. Your credit rating does affect how the lender will view your LTV. A lender may allow a higher than 80 percent LTV to a borrower with an excellent credit rating, while the lender will probably allow a much lower LTV to a customer with less stellar credit.

183. Lenders clearly look at your income, but if your expenses are a large proportion of your earnings, your loan may not be as large or your rates may not be as low as you would like.

184. House payments (principal, interest, tax, and insurance, or "PITI") and your miscellaneous other debt should be below 36 percent of your gross monthly income.

185. Your PITI alone should be no more than 28 percent of your gross monthly income.

186. If you are considering a second mortgage to help purchase the house, the maximum debt-to-income ratio rises to 42 percent, but ask your lender.

187. Although lenders may approve you for loans approaching 42 percent debt-to-income ratios, many people start to become uncomfortable around 38 percent. Talk to your financial planner before committing to increased debt.

188. The LTV determines how much you can borrow overall, while your debt-to-income ratio establishes the monthly payment for which you qualify. Within these two limits you will have a variety of options with different interest rates, loan terms, and points. Shop for the loan that makes the most sense for your needs.

189. Put simply, the less interest you pay, the more loan you can afford. The longer the loan, the lower the monthly payment. But total interest paid is much higher on a longer-term loan.

190. Credit ratings are not static numbers. There are things you can do to develop a solid credit history and improve your credit score.

191. Pay your bills on time consistently. One or two late payments may actually push your credit score to a less desirable number, which may impact your interest rate or terms.

192. Recent late payments, generally in the past twelve months, are more harmful to your credit score than older late payments; so start paying your bills on time today!

193. Pay your largest bills first. The larger the missed or late payment, the more damage it does to your credit rating.

194. Lenders generally look at late payments in descending importance: mortgage payments, car loans, student loans, and credit cards.

195. Try to keep your oldest account active. The oldest account will lengthen your credit history, thus improving your score.

196. Check your credit report once per year. The Fair and Accurate Credit Transactions (FACT) Act of 2003 improved privacy regulations, identified theft protections dispute procedures, and allowed for free annual consumer disclosures. Consumers can request a free copy of their personal consumer disclosure every twelve months from the three largest credit bureaus: TransUnion, Equifax and Experian.

197. Go online for your credit report at annualcreditreport.com.

198. Incorrect information on your credit report can lower your credit score. If there is an error on your credit report, contact the specific creditor to request the correction. If this doesn't work, contact the credit reporting agencies to dispute the record.

199. Negative records such as defaults or bankruptcies remain on your credit report for seven to ten years. With such long-term impact on your credit, be sure to keep your credit spotless.

200. If you are behind on your payments or your account has gone to a collection agency, paying off your debt doesn't immediately remove it from your credit report, but the account will be labeled "paid." This will improve your credit score but not nearly as much as when the record expires in seven to ten years.

201. If you're having trouble making your payments on time, consider automatic payments from your savings account. A strict schedule may keep you out of trouble!

202. Don't max out your credit cards. Your account balances should be below 75 percent of your available credit. This will impact your credit score as well.

203. Don't have too many open lines of credit. Unused credit is a potential red flag to lenders, it is a place you can rack up instant debt if you are already pre-approved.

204. You may be tempted to buy that new couch or plasma TV that's on sale—it will look perfect in your new family room. Hold off on any large purchases until the keys to the house are in your hand! Many lenders pull a second credit report just prior to closing.

205. Avoid too many "hard" inquiries into your credit. When you apply for a new credit card or loan, creditors and lenders initiate hard inquires into your credit. Multiple hard inquires are a signal that you are possibly building your debt potential which can make you a more risky borrower. Hard inquiries into your credit knock your credit score back by a few points.

206. Hard inquires of the same type around the same time—shopping around for mortgages when purchasing a house—are lumped together. The reduction of your FICO score is somewhat less than if those same inquiries where spread over a period of months. You can generally shop mortgage companies within a thirty-day grace period with very little damage to your score.

207. If you are shopping around for mortgages, each lender will be aware that you are talking to other lenders since the competitor lender's inquiry will appear in your credit report; so don't tell a mortgage representative you are not shopping around if you really are.

208. Feel free to check your own credit; such a "soft inquiry" does not harm your FICO score.

209. Cancelling old credit cards can actually lower your credit score by making your credit history appear shorter. Consider closing your new accounts rather than your older accounts.

210. A better way to reduce your levels of available credit is to request a reduction in your credit limits.

211. If you are consolidating your credit balances onto one card, be careful not to have your newly consolidated balance go above 50 percent of that card's credit limit. You don't want the appearance of maxing out a card, which will hurt your credit score.

212. A good rule of thumb is this: the purchase price of the home should be about two-and-one-half times the borrower's annual salary.

213. As part of your FICO score, lenders look at your future home's loan-to-value ratio by dividing the mortgage amount by the property's value. Lenders find loan-to-value ratio above 80 percent more risky, and generally charge higher interest rates.

214. Lenders also look at your debt-to-income ratio by adding all of your monthly debts and dividing by your monthly income. Depending on the lender, ratios of 20 percent to 39 percent or less are thought to be the best credit risks. If your ratio is above that range, lenders tend to charge higher rates.

215. Remember if you co-signed a loan or credit card with a college roommate, former spouse, child, or family member, whatever account you co-signed will appear on your credit report, as well as theirs. If the account is past due, riddled with late payments, etc., it will negatively impact your credit score.

216. The amount of debt remaining on a loan or credit card you co-signed will also be included in your debt totals.

217. The good news on co-signed loans is that if the party you have co-signed with is paying the loan or credit cards consistently on time, it will have a positive impact on your credit score.

218. If you are being negatively impacted by a loan or credit card that you co-signed for, there are two ways to remove yourself from the debt. Either the loan needs to be refinanced without your name attached, or you must petition the creditor to officially remove you from the account.

219. Unfortunately, there is no cure-all to improve your credit score. The two most important factors to improve your credit rating are responsible financial behavior and time.

220. Lenders like to see a consistent job history. If you are changing jobs in the same field, lenders will overlook it; but if you float from job to job, try to stay put to show stability.

Preapproval: An Important Step

221. One of the first, and possibly the most important steps in your home search is to talk to a mortgage representative to see how large a mortgage you will be preapproved for. This will tell you exactly how much money you can spend on a house. If you skip this step, you may be looking at houses that are much more than you can afford, or less expensive than the one you want.

222. The mortgage preapproval is a great tool to have early in your home search. Most sellers expect to see a written copy along with your offer. If you happen to find your dream home in your first few days of looking, you won't have to scramble to get your preapproval.

223. Prequalification and preapproval are not the same thing. Prequalification means that a lender has reviewed the information you have shared with them verbally or online, and considers you qualified to borrow a certain amount of money.

224. Preapproval means that you have supplied specific financial documents such as pay stubs, savings and investment statements, etc., and based on the lender's review of those documents, you have been approved for a loan of a certain amount pending appraisal of the property you intend to purchase.

225. Prequalification may be a great first step for you to figure out what you think you can afford. Most sellers expect a preapproval form accompanying an offer, so you will eventually need to take the more formal steps for a preapproval.

226. Prequalifications generally do not have application fees. Lenders typically charge a fee for a preapproval or when it comes time to actually apply.

227. If you are buying a house with all cash and no mortgage, don't be surprised if a seller asks for a preapproval anyway. If the buyer decides to go on a spending spree before the closing, the seller will want the security that a buyer is still preapproved for a mortgage and can complete the transaction. Also, the seller may want verification that the buyer has adequate cash to complete the transaction. This can be in the form of bank and investment savings or a letter from the buyer's investment company.

228. Even buyers with bad credit histories may be able to get a mortgage. There are literally hundreds of mortgage types and lenders in the U.S. Many specialize in lending to high-risk buyers.

229. If you currently own real estate, have a local agent give you a pricing opinion on its potential market value. It will give you a good idea of how much cash you'll end up with after the sale or how much equity you've built.

230. Pricing options from real estate agents are free and at no obligation. It's also a good way to test out local agents in case you do decide to sell.

231. If you are considering a home equity loan on the property you plan to sell, talk to your lender first. Many don't allow loans on properties currently on the market or allow a smaller portion of the equity to be borrowed against once the property is listed.

232. One thing all loans have in common is fees—sometimes a lot of fees, adding up to hundreds of dollars. While fees vary from lender to lender and loan to loan, most lenders will charge borrowers an application fee, an appraisal fee, and a credit report fee. These fees may be itemized or lumped together.

233. All mortgages have another thing in common: they use the home you are purchasing as collateral. With your home as collateral, you'll want to make sure you do not default on this loan. You can lose your house.

234. Not all lenders call their fees by the same name, which makes comparisons difficult. Ask lenders to quote all of the fees they will be charging you. Ask for an exact definition of each fee. You will be able to compare fees from various lenders even if they are called by different names. Negotiate where possible.

235. Negotiate ahead of time; it could save you hundreds of dollars! Compare your lender's closing costs to others you have had quoted. Look at, and ask for discounts or waivers on, such items as document preparation fee, processing fee, underwriting fee, warehousing fee, appraisal review fee, notary fee, and courier fees.

236. Once you've signed the application and paid the application fee, it is too late to negotiate the other fees. You've got a contract.

237. Federal Truth-in-Lending laws require that lenders provide all closing costs, all fees, and the annual percentage rate (APR) within three days of receiving a borrower's application.

238. Lenders are obligated to disclose finance charges, payment schedules, late charges, and prepayment penalties.

239. Some states allow prepayment penalties for borrowers paying off the loan before the expiration date. While most allow additional payments, lenders may not allow you to completely pay off the loan early. Some loans have prepayment penalties if you pay off the loan in less than five years, but no penalty for prepayment after five years.

240. If you have a mortgage with a pre-payment penalty and decide to move while the penalty is in effect, you will be required to pay the penalty at the time of closing on your sale. The penalty is usually a specified percentage of your loan amount.

241. APR is actually higher than the interest rate you have been quoted because it includes all fees included in the loan. APR can be a great way to compare lender's options, but remember to compare lender fees that are included in the APR.

242. Your parents may insist that thirty-year fixed mortgages are the way to go. They may work for you; they may not. Don't choose a specific mortgage type because somebody told you to. There are now literally hundreds of different lending options available and several may be right for you.

243. You'll hear lots of terms thrown around when looking for a mortgage, one of which is Fannie Mae. Fannie Mae is a private, shareholder-owned company that does not lend money directly to homebuyers. Fannie Mae purchases mortgages from lenders, thus providing the funds necessary for millions of mortgages. Fannie Mae is the nation's largest mortgage purchaser.

244. Fannie Mae—originally called Federal National Mortgage Association (FNMA)—sells government guaranteed FNMA bonds at market rate to raise the necessary funds to purchase mortgages.

245. Mortgage bankers originate loans and sell them to FNMS but retain the servicing function, for which Fannie Mae pays them a fee. What this really means is that you deal face-to-face with the lender, but the actual money comes from Fannie Mae.

246. Freddie Mac (the Federal Home Loan Mortgage Corporation) provides a secondary market for savings and loan associations, mortgage loans, and conventional mortgages. Freddie Mac purchases mortgages, pools them together, and sells bonds using mortgages as security, raising the money that home-buyers use to purchase their real estate.

247. Ginnie Mae is a government corporation formed to assist with low and moderate income and high-risk loans.

248. Conventional loans are arranged entirely between the borrower and lender. Lenders set their own standards as long as they work within national banking regulations.

249. Jumbo loans are loans that are higher than the secondary markets Fannie Mae or Freddie Mac will secure. Mortages below $359,650 are "conventional" mortgages, mortgages above $359,650 are "jumbo." The limit for what constitutes a jumbo loan increases periodically, so check with your lender for any updates. There are more fees for jumbo loans and the interest rates are usually higher than for conventional mortgages.

250. Assumable mortgages enable the buyer to take over the seller's mortgage on the property, paying the same interest rate, making the same monthly payments, and having the same finishing date.

251. Conventional mortgages are not assumable. They are written with a due-on-sale clause meaning that when the property is sold, the mortgage must be paid in full.

252. Federal Housing Administration (FHA) mortgages are assumable. Depending where mortgage rates are at the time of purchase, the rates on the assumed loan could be much lower than the current rates with lower closing costs, translating into potential savings.

Fixed Mortgage

253. Fixed rate mortgages have set mortgage rates that do not change over the life of the loan. As a result, the monthly mortgage payment remains constant through the life of the loan.

254. Just because a fixed rate mortgage payment doesn't vary over time, don't think your total monthly payment won't. Your property taxes and homeowners insurance may be paid along with your mortgage payment, those two items will probably increase over time and increase your total monthly payment.

255. Interest rates on fixed loans tend to be slightly higher than other lending options since lenders will not benefit from possible future increases in prevailing interest rates. Rates on fixed rate loans can be 1 percent or more than variable rate loans.

256. Fixed rate loans are still the most common home loans due to their stable payment plans and interest rates. Remember that interest rates in the 1980s were in the teens, and as recently as 2000, rates were at 8 percent. Increases in interest rates can and do happen—a good point to remember when shopping for mortgages.

257. Fifteen- and thirty-year loans are the most popular fixed rate loans; the deciding factor is generally the monthly payment. A shorter loan will have a higher monthly payment, but the shorter loan life reduces the total loan interest payment.

258. The shorter the term of the fixed rate mortgage year, the lower the interest rate. Even if you pay down a thirty-year fixed mortgage in ten years, you have paid more interest on the shortened thirty-year loan due to the higher interest rates than you would have paid had you initially borrowed on a ten-year loan.

259. Talk to your tax preparer or financial planner when deciding between various mortgage lengths. Because interest payments on mortgages are tax deductible, your financial professional may actually encourage you to select a longer mortgage rather than a shorter one.

260. Borrowers approaching retirement may want to consider shorter fixed rate mortgages instead of the longer ones. With fewer income earning years ahead of you, you may want to utilize your earning power now to pay down your loan rather than during your retirement years.

261. Borrowers in their initial earning years may want a thirty-year fixed mortgage since there are ideally many income earning years ahead of them. The savings from the somewhat lower interest rates can potentially be used for other monthly savings or investments that pay a greater annual return than the percentage difference between the two mortgages they are considering.

262. Borrowers who have limited or fixed incomes generally benefit the most from fixed rate mortgages. Since the interest rate remains steady throughout the entire mortgage, there is no risk of mortgage payments increasing during the life of the loan.

263. People who will simply sleep better at night knowing that their mortgage rate will not increase over the duration of the loan are also ideal users of fixed rate mortgages.

Adjustable Mortgage

264. Adjustable rate mortgages (ARMs) start with a lower initial interest rate, but have the potential to either increase or decrease after a certain time period has elapsed.

265. Lower interest rates in the mortgage market make ARMs more appealing since their initial interest rates are even lower than fixed rate mortgages.

266. Unlike fixed rate mortgages, ARMs, by definition, can increase in interest rate; therefore, payment fluctuates throughout the life of the loan.

267. ARMs come in a few variations: one-, five-, and seven-year adjustable rate mortgages. The interest rate on a five to one variable rate mortgage means it has a fixed rate for five years and then is adjusted annually, based on a lending benchmark such as the prime rate.

268. Borrowers who already have a substantial level of debt via credit cards, student loans, and car loans may reap the most benefits from ARMs. The lower interest rates of ARMs will help keep the collective debt payments from reaching a threshold that lenders find risky: usually around 36 percent to 40 percent of annual income.

269. ARMs can be risky for borrowers planning to stay in their homes for more than ten years. Interest rates are bound to rise sometime during a ten-year period and will effect the borrower's monthly payments.

270. ARMs usually have a cap on how much they can vary, usually 2 percent annually. They also generally cannot jump higher than 5 to 6 percent during the lifetime of the loan. A 2 percent jump can greatly change your monthly payment, let alone a 5 to 6 percent increase. Remember, your rates and caps may be different; so know exactly what changes are allowed in your loan.

271. The initial lower interest rates on an ARM can make an expensive house more affordable to a borrower than a fixed rate mortgage can; however, the rates and monthly payments on an ARM can increase, potentially to a level higher than the fixed rate loans you are being quoted today. If you don't feel you can afford the potentially increased ARM payments, you may want to consider buying a less expensive house.

Interest-Only Loans

272. An interest-only loan is a type of adjustable rate mortgage in which only the interest is due during an initial preset period. The interest-only loan and the ARM of the same amount will have approximately the same interest payment. The ARM will also have portions of the principal due each month, while the interest-only loan will not. Obviously, this greatly reduces the monthly payment due on the interest-only loan.

273. After the initial preset time has expired, the interest rate will become adjustable and portions of the principal will also become payable, both potentially increasing the monthly payment dramatically. Ask your mortgage representative what scenarios are possible with your specific loan.

274. Because the initial period of an interest-only loan does not include payments to principal, once the principal payments are due, the payments are amortized on the remaining life of the loan. A five-year interest-only loan has principal payments calculated on the remaining twenty-five years rather than the original thirty-year term.

275. Negative amortization is an option used to help lessen monthly payments in an interest-only loan. If a borrower chooses negative amortization, the monthly payment is actually less than the interest due. This can be a risky undertaking since it essentially causes your loan balance to increase rather than decrease. While your payments might be lower now, over time, they will grow.

276. Interest-only loans work best for borrowers who have the flexibility and discipline to invest the money they are saving during the interest-only period. Investment profits should ideally cover the monthly increase when the loan's principal becomes due.

277. Interest-only mortgages are also a good option for self-employed people with profitable businesses. By investing the monthly savings into their business, there will ideally be returns greater than the rate of their loan. As always, talk this over with your financial planner.

278. To avoid the sharp increase in payments on an interest-only mortgage, borrowers can refinance the loans before they've adjusted. Ideally, interest rates on other mortgage options have not climbed dramatically, and the balance owed can be financed into a more stable loan style.

No Money Down

279. No money down loans allow borrowers to purchase a home without liquidating assets for a down payment.

280. No money down, or no down payment loans, are usually available to borrowers with very high credit scores or the assets to cover the loan.

281. Remember that any mortgage over 80 percent of the property's value must be covered by Private Mortgage Insurance (PMI). Consider those non-tax deductible payments, particularly when considering this loan type.

Federal Housing Administration (FHA) Loans

282. FHA loans can enable borrowers to place as little as 3 percent down. This enables buyers with a shortage of down payment funds to buy a home.

283. The FHA does not make loans; it insures lenders against defaults by borrowers. As with any loan, your credit history and income will be looked at before you qualify.

284. A common misconception is that FHA loans have an income maximum. There are no income maximums and you do not have to be a first-time buyer to qualify.

Biweekly and Other Mortgage Types

285. Biweekly mortgages have one advantage over traditional monthly mortgages—the biweekly payment schedule equates to twenty-six payments annually versus twelve. In essence, the borrower is making thirteen monthly payments in one year, thereby paying down the mortgage more quickly.

286. Biweekly mortgages force the borrower into a biweekly payment plan with penalties for late payments. If your finances are touch-and-go, you may not want a rigid, every-two-weeks payment plan.

287. Most mortgages allow for extra payments throughout the life of the mortgage. You can get the same interest savings by making the equivalent of thirteen monthly payments (or more!) on your own timing. This allows for extra payments during flush times, after holiday bonuses for example, but only monthly payments during normal times.

288. 80/10/10 and 80/15/5 loans are actually two mortgages taken at the same time. With an 80/10/10, the first mortgage is for 80 percent of the price, 10 percent second mortgage, and 10 percent down. Both mortgages are usually from the same lender. 80/10/10 and 80/15/5 loans allow borrowers to finance 90 percent to 95 percent of the purchase price without paying private mortgage insurance.

289. The interest rate on the second mortgage of an 80/10/10 or 80/15/5 loan is usually around 2 percent higher than the first mortgage. The loans are usually due in fifteen years, but the payments are amortized over thirty years, keeping the monthly payment lower.

290. The interest paid on the second mortgage in these types of loans is tax deductible, which means great savings for you!

291. Make sure your second loan does not have a prepayment penalty. Because second loans generally have a higher interest rate, you may choose to pay them off first; so make sure you are not penalized for prepayment.

292. Be careful, because the balance of the second mortgage, though amortized over thirty years, is actually due at the end of fifteen years! Chances are you will have moved or refinanced by then.

293. Two–step mortgages are available in at least two versions, both of which are thirty-year loans. 5/25 mortgages have a fixed interest rate for the first five years at which point the mortgage can be converted to a twenty-five-year fixed rate mortgage or a one-year adjustable mortgage. A 7/23 mortgage has a fixed rate for the first seven years and then can be converted to a twenty-three-year fixed mortgage or a one-year adjustable mortgage.

294. Obviously there is more risk to a borrower in a two-step mortgage than in a traditional fixed mortgage; prevailing mortgage rates could increase during the initial fixed rate period. Two-steps are less risky than an ARM loan, which could increase in rate during the entire loan period. Because of that, interest rates on two-step loans are usually lower than thirty-year fixed mortgages and higher than ARM loans.

295. Borrowers who plan to move or refinance in fewer than five or seven years benefit from Two-step mortgages by paying low interest rates for the first five or seven years. Depending where rates are at the end of five or seven years, holding on to the loan even past that period may save the borrower in overall interest payments.

296. If you are a qualified veteran, consider a VA loan, which is administered by the federal Department of Veteran Affairs (VA). VA loans are designed to allow little or no money down and have no points. One restriction is that the veteran using a VA loan must occupy the house as her primary residence.

297. Veteran's closing costs are limited by VA; so the costs may be picked up by the seller, which are a savings to the buyer and a cost to the seller. Sellers may be reluctant to sell to a buyer using a VA loan for that reason.

298. A VA loan is not limited to first-time buyers. A qualified borrower can use her benefits several times as long as the house being purchased is her primary residence.

299. A common misconception is that the VA sets the interest rates on a VA loan. The lender actually sets the interest rate. As with all loans, it pays to shop around for the best rates and terms.

300. Balloon mortgages are amortized over a preset period, generally fifteen to thirty years. Borrowers make regular payments of principal and interest, or interest only, until the end of the loan, which is a much shorter period of, say, five years. At the end of the loan, the large balance is due, which is called the balloon payment because of its size.

301. Balloon mortgages make the monthly payments much more manageable, but borrowers need to be careful and remember that the lump sum is due at the end of the fairly short loan period. If rates have increased dramatically during the term of the loan, a new loan to cover that balloon payment may be costly.

302. Shared-appreciation mortgages are primarily designed to help low-income first-time homebuyers afford homes. In exchange for below-market rate loans, borrowers agree to share an agreed-to percentage of any appreciation or profit made on the house with the lender.

303. Borrowers may be tempted to use a shared-appreciation loan initially to purchase a home and pay off the loan early to avoid sharing appreciation. Shared appreciation loans have prepayment penalties to discourage this tactic, so check with your lender up front.

304. One bonus of the shared appreciation loan is that if your house doesn't appreciate by the time you sell it, your lender doesn't make any money either (outside of the interest you've already paid)!

305. It's not just market conditions driving up the value of your home that you will need to share with your lender. Some lenders expect to receive the same agreed-to level of profit sharing from any upgrades or renovations you choose to make while living in the home. So be careful; you'll be sharing the increased value on your home for the family room you decide to add. Make sure you thoroughly understand your loan rules before you sign on the dotted line!

306. Also remember if you remain in the house at the end of a shared appreciation loan, you'll need cash to pay your lender their portion of the appreciation on the property!

307. Read your loan terms carefully; if you sell your house shortly after moving in, the lender may charge penalties exceeding the price you can get for the house!

308. BC mortgages are available to borrowers who have less than stellar credit. BC refers to any borrower who has less than "A" credit.

309. For most mortgage holders, the interest paid in one month is actually for the previous month, not the current month. You are paying in what is called arrears, meaning if you close on your loan on May 15, you would pay for the half month of interest from May 1–15, but not pay June's interest until July 1.

310. For anyone who has less than exemplary credit, it is more likely that you will have to prepay your interest. In sub-prime loans, or BC loans, you are actually paying June's interest on June 1, not July 1.

311. People who have been self-employed for just a short period of time want a no documentation loan; or those who have had a spotty job history, may be the ideal candidates for a BC mortgage.

312. No documentation loans, or "no doc" are so called because they require almost no documentation. Because no doc borrowers are bigger risks to lenders, interest rates can be considerably higher.

313. Private Mortgage Insurance, or PMI, is required by the lender if the borrower has put less than 20 percent down. The borrower pays for the PMI, which protects the lender, not the borrower, in the case of foreclosure. The lower the down payment, the higher the PMI costs, especially where the down payment is under 5 percent.

314. States generally regulate PMI requirements. Most states mandate that lenders require PMI on loans with less than 20 percent down.

315. Virtually any borrower who has a down payment of less than 20 percent will have to pay PMI in the case of a private lender loan, or FHA mortgage insurance on FHA loans with less than 20 percent down.

316. Unlike interest on a mortgage, PMI payments are not tax deductible.

317. The Homeowners Protection Act of 1998 says that for mortgages signed on or after July 29, 1999, PMI must be terminated automatically when borrowers reach 22 percent equity of the home's original property value.

318. The same law mandates that PMI also can be cancelled, at the borrower's request when the borrower reaches 20 percent equity of the home's original property value. You'll want to pay attention to your mortgage statements to see when you've reached that 20 percent equity level; it could save you multiple PMI payments.

319. At the loan closing, lenders must tell borrowers exactly when loan payments will bring the borrower up to 20 percent equity level. This timetable assumes no increase in value of the home. Depending on market conditions, chances are good that the home will indeed increase in the value before the stated date.

320. The borrower can also hire an appraiser to determine the value of the property. If the borrower has reached 20 percent equity level, the lender must cancel PMI.

321. Borrowers can opt to include PMI costs in the loan by working with the lender to include the costs in a higher interest rate. The only way to eliminate the PMI cost is to refinance the entire loan.

322. Borrowers of FHA loans who have put down less than 20 percent are required to pay for mortgage insurance or MI, which is the government version of PMI. Unlike PMI, you cannot cancel MI even after reaching 20 percent equity. In order to eliminate MI, borrowers must refinance their FHA loan into a conventional loan.

Tips for Taking a Mortgage

323. Monitor interest rates. Mortgage rates fluctuate almost daily. You'll want to monitor the rates as your mortgage "lock-in" date approaches.

324. Borrowers can gamble that mortgage rates are going to decrease between the time of the application and the time of the closing. This is called "floating." Borrowers will eventually need to "lock-in" a mortgage rate, meaning they agree to take a mortgage at that specific rate.

325. Lock-in periods are usually less than sixty days, meaning the rate is guaranteed for sixty days after which the rate can increase or decrease. Lenders do not like exceptionally long lock-in periods because it reduces the likelihood that the borrower will pay increased rates.

326. The longer the lock-in period, the higher fee you will pay. If you think you will be closing in thirty-five days, take a forty-day lock-in, not a sixty-day lock-in.

327. For the risk averse, consider taking a mortgage with a rate that is already locked-in. This will keep you from sweating the rate changes each day.

328. Be careful of points and fees! Lenders have many different options, and they may all have different points and fees attached to them.

329. The more points you pay, the lower your interest rate will be, in general. A point is 1 percent of the total loan amount, which is paid as a one-time fee to the lender for the lower rate. The point is on top of whatever mortgage amount you are taking and is paid at closing.

330. Points are tax deductible; always ask your tax preparer about this.

331. You can negotiate with your lender for lower fees, fewer points, or a lower interest rate if you are borrowing a substantial amount of money, have excellent credit, or the mortgage market is competitive. It can't hurt to ask!

332. Shop around. With so many lenders, you can pit lender versus lender. If one lender is offering a lower rate, ask another lender to beat or match it!

333. Lenders can reject you for inconsistencies on your application, so be honest. Don't say your income is $80,000 when it's really $50,000. If you don't know the answer to an application question, don't make up an answer. Lenders can reject you for discrepancies that are large or small, so honesty is the best policy.

334. If you are making a lateral job move for more money in the same industry or moving up the corporate ladder to the next level, lenders will be happy to see the job switch. If you are moving from industry to industry, the lender will view this behavior as unstable and may reject your application.

335. If you are self-employed, lenders typically like to see that you have been at that same job for at least two years. The same goes for borrowers whose incomes rely heavily on commissions.

336. Lenders will usually ask for a self-employed borrower's last two tax returns and/or profit/loss statements. Lenders are more interested in the borrower's net income than the gross income.

Mortgage Snafus

What happens if the mortgage you were so carefully counting on goes awry? In this section I'll explain how to handle issues like what to do if your mortgage application is rejected or if your house appraises for less than the purchase price. Believe it or not, you do still have options.

What to Do If Your Mortgage Application Is Denied

337. Your lender has up to thirty days from the date of your completed application to inform you if your mortgage loan has been approved.

338. If your application is rejected, the lender must tell you in writing.

339. If your mortgage is denied, you have up to sixty days to ask the lender why you were rejected. The lender must inform you of the reasons why your application was denied.

340. The lender must be specific about the reason for your rejection. Insufficient income or short employment history are acceptable responses. "You didn't meet our minimum standards" is not a specific enough answer.

341. If you have less than stellar credit or a spotty employment history, all hope is not lost. B and C loans are generally available to borrowers considered more risky. To cover their risk, lenders typically charge much higher interest rates than they would to "A" customers.

What to Do If Your Mortgage Appraisal Is Less Than Your Purchase Price

342. If the property you are purchasing does not appraise at purchase price, and you are making a deposit of 20 percent or less, your lender is unlikely to give you a mortgage for the amount you are asking for.

343. As part of the mortgage contingency, chances are the buyer can cancel the deal. Since the house did not appraise at purchase price, the buyer's mortgage may not be approved. The most common solution is for the seller to reduce the price accordingly.

344. A cash buyer should also be protected by a contingency clause that states he can cancel the deal if the home doesn't appraise at or above the sales price. Read your contract before signing.

345. Ask the lender to send out another appraiser if you feel the appraisal is incorrect. Sometimes appraisers look at incorrect comps, or merely do a drive-by appraisal. If the house you are purchasing has many interior upgrades, they may have been overlooked. The lender may send out a new home appraiser or ask the original appraiser to reevaluate the property.

346. The buyer can also consider making up the difference by putting more cash down, or the seller and buyer can compromise at a new price.

Know Your Rights

347. Federal law protects you against discrimination when you apply for a mortgage to purchase, refinance, or make home improvements.

348. The Equal Credit Opportunity Act prohibits discrimination in any aspect of a credit transaction based on race, color, religion, national origin, sex, marital status, or age.

349. The Fair Housing Act bans engaging in the following practices based on race, color, national origin, religion, sex, familial status or handicap (disability):

- Refusal to make a mortgage loan
- Refusal to provide information regarding loans
- Imposition of different terms or conditions on a loan, such as different interest rates, points, or fees
- Discrimination in appraising property
- Refusal to purchase a loan or set different terms or conditions for purchasing a loan

350. A borrower's bill of rights—Article Z of the federal Truth in Lending Act—requires lenders to disclose interest rates, terms, costs, and variable-rate features in a total Annual Percentage Rate (APR). This information makes it easier for borrowers to compare lenders and loan costs.

351. If a mortgage lender does not disclose the APR, application fees must be refunded.

352. If any loan terms change before closing, and you decide to cancel your loan application, the lender must return all fees.

353. Borrowers have three days from the day of closing to cancel an application. Borrowers must inform the lender in writing within those three days to have all fees refunded.

354. Lenders must consider reliable public assistance income in the same way as other income.

355. Any income from part-time employment, social security, pensions, and annuities must be considered in the same manner as other income.

356. A lender is allowed to ask you for proof of consistent receipt of alimony, child support, or separate maintenance payments, if you choose to claim these as sources of income.

357. Although lenders cannot consider your race, national origin, or sex, you will be asked to voluntarily disclose this information to help federal agencies enforce anti-discrimination laws.

358. Lenders are allowed to ask about your immigration status to determine whether or not you have the right to remain in the country long enough to repay the debt.

359. The racial profile of the neighborhood cannot be considered by the lender during the application process or as part of the appraisal.

360. Although lenders cannot discriminate regarding a borrower having or not having children, lenders may ask about expenses related to your dependents.

361. Lenders cannot require a co-signer if you meet the lender's standards.

362. Redlining is the refusal by mortgage lenders or insurers to issue loans or policies for a specific geographical area. Antidiscrimination laws make redlining illegal.

363. Many states make it illegal to charge borrowers fees or penalties for early payment of mortgages. Always ask to see this clause on paper even if you think your chances of paying the loan early are slim.

Taxes

Tax Implications

364. Generally the largest tax deduction for a new homeowner is the interest paid on the mortgage. In the first years of any mortgage, the majority of the payment applies toward interest. Interest is generally fully deductible.

365. Current tax law makes the first $250,000 of profit from a home sale for a single person and $500,000 for a married couple tax-free if the seller has lived in the dwelling for at least two years. Selling in less than two years makes the profit taxable, so check with your tax preparer if you think you may live in a home for a shorter period.

366. If you are cashing in stocks, bonds, or mutual funds, there will be federal tax implications. Before you decide to sell an investment to help finance your new home, talk to your financial planner or tax preparer to select the investment with the most favorable tax implications for your specific situation.

367. Penalties for early withdrawal on 401(k) plans can reach 10 percent or more. Unless you can prove hardships such as disability or large amounts of un-reimbursed medical expenses, there are heavy penalties for withdrawal before age fifty-nine and a half. Talk to your financial planner and tax preparer before touching your 401(k).

368. Many 401(k) funds allow you to borrow from the plan. You are actually promising to pay yourself back with interest! The interest rate is usually 1 percent over prime rate.

369. You can usually borrow up to 50 percent of your account total to a maximum of $50,000, and the loan can be taken for a maximum of five years, after which the unpaid balance will be considered an early withdrawal, and penalized accordingly.

370. Also remember that you'll be paying back your pre-tax loan with after-tax dollars. When you eventually retire, you'll be taxed again. You'll have been double taxed on those same post-tax dollars.

371. Many states have a "Millionaire's Tax" or "Mansion Tax." The tax is a percentage of the purchase price of a home that sells over a stated amount. The tax is generally on the entire amount of the purchase price, not just the amount over the stated level. It is a one-time payment due at closing. Ask your realtor, attorney, or tax preparer if such a tax is in effect in your state. And remember, while the tax may be called "millionaire" or "mansion" the purchase price it taxes may not really be for what you would truly consider a mansion.

Property Taxes and Other Costs

372. When moving into a new area, check to see if your car insurance payments will change based on your new address. Include this increased or hopefully decreased cost into you monthly budget.

373. General taxes on property can be levied from various levels of local government: municipal, county, state and even school districts, park districts and water, sanitary or drainage districts. Find out what taxes apply on your new house or condo and consider them in your monthly budget. Tax information should be included with the listing information prepared by the seller's realtor or can be found at the municipality tax office.

374. Certain states or towns have exemptions from real estate taxes. Special groups such as senior citizens and veterans may also be exempt.

375. Areas that are growing rapidly in population tend to have increases in property taxes to pay for all that additional infrastructure new residents will be using, such as roads, sewers, and schools.

376. Special assessment taxes may be levied to specific areas to pay for improvements that will directly benefit those homeowners. Examples include new sewers, new curbs, or new sidewalks being installed in a specific neighborhood.

377. If the schools need to construct new buildings or wings, local taxes will generally increase to cover the new costs. Call the local school board or attend town meetings to find out more.

378. As with the interest paid on your mortgage, property taxes you pay in a given year can be deducted from your gross income to reduce your taxable income.

379. Look at other monthly costs you currently pay and see if your new location will require a change in cost. Things to look at are child care, gym membership, grocery shopping, and commuting costs. Incorporate these adjusted numbers into your monthly budget.

380. Request an estimate of all of your closing costs from your mortgage representative or title representative, whomever is handling your closing. They should be able to estimate the amount of "cash" you'll need to close. This will include all taxes and fees that you'll need to pay.

381. Ask your agent for an estimate of all fees associated with a property, especially a condominium or co-op. Many associations have monthly or quarterly maintenance fees, which will impact your monthly budget.

382. Check to see if there is a "capital fee" or "purchase fee" assessed on the condo or co-op you are planning to buy. Associations sometimes have these one-time fees payable at the time of purchase as a way to replenish the association coffers. These fees can be in the hundreds or even thousands of dollars, so ask before you make your offer.

383. One of the main reasons for down payments is to show the sellers how serious the buyer is about the purchase. A no money down deal may make the seller feel the buyer has little to lose financially if the deal falls apart.

384. Many transactions require two or three deposits prior to closing; ask your realtor or mortgage representative what is typical for your area ahead of time.

385. Check your investments and bank accounts prior to making an offer so you know how liquid or accessible your funds are. You'll want to make sure you can get your money when you need it without penalty.

386. Plan your deposit schedule around when your funds will be liquid and penalty free if possible, or incorporate those penalties as part of your budget.

387. Many lenders look at the monthly tax payments and monthly maintenance fees for condos and co-ops when assessing what a buyer can afford. If you are purchasing a home with high taxes or high maintenance fees, those extra fees may cut into the actual mortgage you are approved for.

More Key Players

388. During your homebuying experience, you'll talk to lots of brokers, agents, representatives, customer service account executives, etc. Remember though that each of these roles can also be called "salesperson." They all make their living selling you their product or service.

389. Independent insurance companies or insurance companies partnering with real estate companies offer home warranty or home protection plans in many areas of the country. The policies can cover homes of almost any age and usually insure major systems such as electrical, heating and cooling, and major appliances such as washers, dryers, and refrigerators. The builder usually covers newly constructed homes separately. Builder warranties typically include systems, appliances, and structural components like the roof and building materials.

390. Home warranties are sometimes paid for by the seller when they list the home, condo, or co-op, or by the buyers when they purchase the property. Check to see who is responsible for the payment.

391. Some states do not regulate home warranties. You'll want to find out if your state regulates home warranties by checking with the state's regulatory division for insurance.

392. Check with the local Better Business Bureau or state attorney general's office to see if the home warranty company has many complaints about unpaid claims. This will be a good indication of whether this home warranty will pay out any claim you may have.

393. Even if the house, condo, or co-op you are buying is not brand new, and even if you are not the first owner, some parts of the structure may be covered by the original builder's warranty. Major structural features such as the roof and foundation as well as major systems such as plumbing and electrical may be covered by the builder for up to ten years, and possibly longer.

394. Ask to see exactly what systems, appliances, and structural conditions are covered by a home warranty. This may save you money on the furnace that looks like it is not going to make it through another winter.

395. Home warranties may cover some of the repairs you are asking for prior to purchase. If they are, there is a better chance your seller will agree to those repairs since the money is not coming out of his pocket.

396. If there is a home warranty on a property you are purchasing, find out how long the warranty lasts and how much it costs to renew. Mark the dates in your calendar so you have no lapse in coverage if you plan to extend it. The lapse in coverage could cost you a higher premium or the cost of repairing an item breaking during that lapse.

397. A home warranty on a house or condo is not necessarily a red flag indicating there are problems with the property. Many sellers choose to include a warranty simply to allay the fears of potential buyers. The warranty reduces the risk that the next homeowner will need to pay for a multitude of repairs soon after purchasing the home.

398. You'll want to have a new survey drawn for your new property. The surveyor will note things like fences, sheds, driveways, and of course, the house and property lines, which are all great information for future projects. You don't want to plant those expensive evergreens in your neighbor's yard instead of your own.

Insurance

Title Insurance: What It Is and Why You Need It

399. Most people have no idea what title insurance is, let alone that there are two types of title insurance policies. Lender's title insurance protects the lender, not the buyer, from title claims, while homeowners title insurance protects the homebuyer.

400. Chances are you'll want both lender's and buyer's insurance. Your lender may insist that you have lender's title insurance. You'll want buyer's title insurance to protect your current and future equity in the home against most major causes of title losses.

401. A lender's title insurance policy protects the lender against title losses due to forged signatures, title claims by heirs and ex-spouses, recording mistakes, errors in deed indexing, title search mistakes, unpaid property taxes and other recorded liens, improper foreclosures, and undisclosed easements.

402. Title insurance is a one-time payment, usually before the closing. The cost is usually based on the sale price of the home.

403. In some areas of the country, the seller pays for the title insurance, not the buyer. Ask your realtor what's customary in your area. Doing so shows that the seller is selling a property with a clean title.

404. Both the lender and the buyer are interested in "good title" or "clean title." The title should be free of any defects, easements, liens, or mortgages other than the one you are taking. This is the information your title company will be investigating.

405. Title searches are not just conducted by title companies and title specialists, they can also be handled by your attorney. Ask your attorney if she will be handling the title search for you.

406. Surprisingly, the most common reason for title insurance problems is forgery. Somewhere in the chain of title is a forged signature, usually an ex-spouse forging the other's signature on the deed.

407. Liens against the property, meaning claims against the property by a person, lender, or tax assessor are fairly common. If work was done to the house but remains unpaid, a contractor may have placed a mechanic's lien against the property. If property taxes remain unpaid, there may be a tax lien against the property.

408. If the current owner hasn't done a thorough title search, liens may exist on the property from before his ownership.

409. Even if you are buying a house or condo from an owner who just purchased the dwelling in the past year or two, you will be required to get a new title policy. The reason being that a new lien or claim may have been placed on the property in the very recent past.

410. Be sure to ask for a discount on title insurance if the property you are buying was purchased in the past two years! If the property changed hands or was refinanced in the past two years, chances are a title search was completed at that time and older title problems would have been uncovered during that search.

411. The cost of a policy of title insurance is based on the purchase price of the dwelling. A higher purchase price generates a higher insurance premium.

412. It's almost more important to use homeowners title insurance if you are purchasing a house, condo, or co-op with cash only. In a cash deal there is no lender to mandate a title search, thus a title problem could remain hidden until after the closing.

413. Buying directly from a builder doesn't mean there may not be a problem with the title. If one of the subcontractors has placed a lien on the property because the builder hasn't paid him, you'll want title insurance to protect you. The same is true if you purchase a "for sale by owner."

414. In comparison to other types of insurance, title insurance rarely pays claims. Most of the premiums paid to title insurers are spent on title research prior to issuing the title policy. This decreases the amount of claims title insurers need to pay out and alerts the buyer to any problems prior to closing.

Protecting Your Investment

415. Homeowners insurance policies consist of property protection and liability protection. Property protection includes coverage for damage to the dwelling itself and its contents. Liability covers the medical claims of people injured on your property.

416. A lot of the time, real estate companies partner with insurance companies and offer competitive rates. Ask the agent you are working with if his company has any affiliations or discounts.

417. Homeowners insurance can vary in price, so don't just choose the first company you contact. Get at least three quotes so you can compare them.

418. Lenders will not care about how much, if any, insurance you get to cover the contents of your house. They're interested only in the value of the dwelling and land, not your personal possessions; so don't ask your lender how much insurance you need. If your condo burns to the ground, lenders do not care if your plasma TV gets replaced.

419. To protect its investment, the lender will require that you have a hazard insurance policy to cover the property against fire. You should also buy a policy that covers personal possessions, liability, vandalism, theft, water damage not caused by flooding, as well as loss of the use of the dwelling.

420. The fact that you are buying a condo or co-op is not a green light to skimp on homeowners insurance. The same perils of vandalism, water damage, and liability affect you as much as a single-family homeowner. Due to close proximity to neighbors, you may be even more affected!

421. Your condo or co-op association will carry insurance to cover common areas of the building or development, and your lender will ask for verification of the policy. Don't be confused. The association's coverage for the common areas does not cover your individual unit. You will need homeowners insurance to cover your unit and its contents.

422. A higher deductible will save you money on your monthly payments. The difference between a $500 deductible and $1,000 deductible can be around 25 percent. Just make sure you can afford the deductible when it comes time for a claim.

423. Consider keeping a separate savings account for or earmarking part of your monthly savings from the increased deductible. This special account can be the emergency fund to cover the deductible in the event of a claim.

424. Most lenders mandate that buyers pay for a full year of homeowners insurance at closing.

425. Different insurers have different payment plans available: monthly, quarterly, etc. Choose the payment plan that best matches your financial plans.

426. Some items such as personal computers, expensive jewelry, or electronics such as home theater systems may not be covered by the standard homeowners policy. Make sure you ask and be sure to insure those expensive personal items not covered by your homeowners. Don't forget about every suit and pair of shoes you own or your CD and MP3 collection.

427. Don't get insurance for the total purchase price of your home. Part of the purchase price was for the land underneath your house. Since land is not subject to theft, fire, etc., there is no reason to pay to insure it.

428. Ask your insurer if there are physical ways to decrease the cost of insurance. Examples would be adding earthquake reinforcement, a new plumbing system, or fire alarms.

429. Consider the type of construction in certain areas of the country. There may be a discount for brick or cement constructed houses in hurricane or tornado prone areas while that same construction may cost you more in earthquake-prone areas. Call your insurer before your search so you know what type of building material may save you money.

430. Homes in more rural areas not offering rapid fire response are generally insured at higher rates than in more developed areas offering quick fire protection. Consider these costs when shopping for your home.

431. Many insurers give a sizable discount on policies for homes with working security systems. In many cases the discount exceeds the monthly fee to the security company. Include this potential savings when you are looking at your monthly budget.

432. Many insurers offer long term customers special discounts for their past loyalty. Find out from your insurer if you qualify for such a discount.

433. Quit smoking! Thousands of homes are destroyed or damaged each year from fires caused by smokers. Homeowners policies charge smokers more than non-smokers.

434. If you are looking at older homes, say built before 1945, check to see what kind of electrical service the house has. Houses with fuse boxes may be more difficult to get fire insurance for. Check with local insurers prior to closing to avoid any last minute problems.

435. Consider purchasing a replacement cost policy. These policies will pay to rebuild your home even if the cost to rebuild exceeds your policy limit. Payment caps vary from company to company; so always ask the insurer while you are collecting quotes. Some companies will pay a claim up to the policy limit while others will pay up to 120 percent or 125 percent of the policy limit.

436. Replacement insurance is generally based on the square footage that the appraiser provided. Ask for a copy of the appraiser's report and have a contractor double check the square footage.

437. Some insurers will give a low estimate of replacement costs in order to save you money. This may help keep your premiums low, but it can cost you a lot of money if your dwelling ever needs to be replaced.

438. Make sure your policy has an enforcement to code provision (or ordinance or code upgrade provision). If a tree causes damage to part of your roof, your municipality may require that you replace the entire roof in order to bring it up to current standards. You want to make sure your insurance covers the cost of bringing the repairs up to code, not just the three-foot hole caused by the tree.

439. Ask for inflation protection on your insurance policy. You'll want your policy to automatically increase as the cost of living increases over time.

440. Even if this is your primary residence, make sure your policy covers the dwelling if you are absent for an extended period of time. If you winter each year in Tahiti for a month or two, make sure your policy covers your home while you are away.

441. Seriously consider "windstorm" damage insurance if you live in a hurricane-frequented area of the country. Pay careful attention to the "hurricane" deductible since it is most likely much higher than other deductibles in your policy.

442. Homeowners policies cover damage from basic to more encompassing causes. Look at the list of causes covered in your policy and compare your quotes accordingly. Make sure you are comfortable with the risks of the causes not covered in your policy.

443. Credit history doesn't just affect your mortgage rates. Many insurers believe that the better your credit history, the less likely you are to file an insurance claim. Insurers are looking for a history of consistent, timely payments to demonstrate responsibility and a lower likelihood of insurance claims.

3.

Finding the Right Type of Home for You

When buying a home, most of us immediately think of a house. Don't rule out your other options though. Learn the differences between houses, condominiums, co-operatives, and town-houses. If you like the idea of owning your own home but are concerned with the amount of upkeep a house requires, there are certainly options that will give you what you desire without the added work. Are you the right person for a fixer-upper, or do you prefer new construction? Learn all of your options and the pros and cons of each.

Condos and Co-ops: The Difference

444. A condominium is a style of ownership, not a style of housing. Condominium ownership is individual ownership of a unit in a multiunit building or unit built on land owned in common. Each condo owner owns a certain percentage of the total building or land including common areas such as lobbies, hallways, and lawns.

445. Each condo unit will have its own block and lot number similar to a single family home.

446. A condominium apartment or townhouse is "real" property. Owners receive a deed similar to one for a single-family house. In a condo, you usually do not own the exterior. Buyers usually own the space within the walls ("sheetrock to sheetrock") and from floor to ceiling.

447. Roofs and foundations are normally the responsibility of the condo association, but windows and exterior doors are usually the owner's responsibility. Always ask first so you know what your financial responsibilities will be.

448. Each individual condominium in a building or complex receives its own tax bill. That tax is tax deductible on your federal income taxes, but check on this with your tax preparer.

449. Some lenders will not issue mortgages to buildings or developments that have less than 70 percent owner-occupied units. Ask your realtor to find out if the complex you are interested in has a lot of renters.

450. Condo buildings or developments with heavy concentrations of renters can have the tendency to have maintenance issues due to the lack of on-site owners and the potential to lose value.

451. "Townhouse" may sometimes be used interchangeably with "condominium," but a townhouse is a housing style, not a type of ownership. It is usually a multistory unit with an exterior entry and a common wall shared with a neighbor(s).

452. Co-operative or co-op is another type of ownership. The building or complex is owned by a corporation. Buyers own shares in the corporation, not their actual unit. The number of shares purchased is usually tied directly to the size or value of the unit you are purchasing. The shares in the co-operative are what give the purchaser the right to live in the unit.

453. Co-operative ownership is an older form of ownership than condominium ownership. It is popular in some larger cities such as New York and Chicago, but pretty rare in the rest of the country.

454. Technically, owners in co-ops do not own real estate, which is land and/or improvements on land; they own stock.

455. A disadvantage to buying into a co-op is that if enough owners do not pay their monthly assessments the corporation may run into financial troubles.

456. In most instances, if the corporation is sold through foreclosure the shares owned in it become almost valueless, even to owners who have paid all of their financial obligations to the corporation.

457. Ask for information regarding the reserves held by the corporation. This fund is meant for future repairs and emergency payments and acts as a buffer to financial default by the corporation.

458. Monthly maintenance fees cover building or complex expenses for insurance, taxes, corporation mortgage payments, and sometimes utilities.

459. Part of the monthly maintenance fees are tax deductible. Verify with your tax preparer that the portion of your fee earmarked for paying the corporations mortgage and taxes is tax deductible, which is usually the case.

460. Condo owners may sell their units to whomever they choose without any type of board review or approval. Co-op associations, or boards, reserve the right to review all applications of potential purchasers.

461. In addition to background checks and financial reviews, some co-ops insist on meeting applicants' children, pets, and even domestic employees!

462. Co-op boards cannot reject you for reasons based on race, religion, or gender, but they can reject you for financial, safety, or "personal" reasons.

463. Both owners of condos and co-ops are bound by bylaws of the homeowners association.

464. Ask for a copy of the co-op rules prior to making your offer. Many co-ops forbid renting out co-ops, allowing grown children to live in the unit, or the owner using the unit as a part-time home rather than a primary residence.

465. At the beginning of your search, if you can't decide whether condo, co-op, or single family ownership is right for you, why not see a sampling of each that fall into your price range? It will enable you to make a more educated decision.

466. Just because you've decided to purchase a condo or co-op, it doesn't mean you don't need a home inspection. Although you only own your unit or co-op shares, potential problems could exist within the space you are responsible for. You'll want to know before you move in!

467. A good home inspector hired to review a condo or co-op will take a look at common areas as well. He may be able to give you a heads up on potential problems in the common areas that may soon effect your maintenance payments.

New Construction

468. Many new developments have sales offices. They are great places to get information on the development from neighborhood maps, house floor plans, lists of amenities, etc. You usually have to sign yourself in while at the sales office. If you want a buyer's broker to represent you, make sure you sign in using your agent's name. If you don't, chances are you will not be allowed to use that agent to represent you during the process.

469. If you elect to have one of the selling agents from the sales office represent you, find out if they are representing you or the seller. Get that information on paper.

470. Builders typically have selling commissions built into their price. If you choose not to use a buying broker, the builder will usually pocket the savings. Rarely will the builder pass the savings along to you.

471. Don't be surprised if you pay much more than the advertised "starting at" price you saw in the local paper. That house is the bare bones model with no options and on the least desirable lot. It is quite easy to spend tens of thousands of dollars on upgrades in new construction. Have a preset limit in mind before you offer on new construction.

472. Many upgrades make sense to do while the house is still in construction. You may not want to reopen the newly sheet-rocked walls after you move in to install new lighting or electrical outlets. Just be careful of overspending! Compare the upgrade costs offered by the builder to what a contractor will charge post-construction. Contractor costs may actually come in lower!

473. You may want a new house and not a "used" house. You will probably be paying a premium for that newness. New houses will generally cost more than a fairly identical pre-owned house half a mile away.

474. New developments or neighborhoods built by builders are generally on the outer edges of suburbs. Builders prefer large tracts of open land, but most of this is already developed in cities and inner suburbs. "Spot" building, "infill," or "spec" houses are usually built a handful at a time in cities and inner suburbs.

475. Spec homes that are already complete can be a good deal if they have been on the market for a while. The builder's goal is to build and sell as quickly as possible. Days on the market cost the developer money, so there may be some negotiability.

476. When builders are developing large tracts farther afield, shopping, schools, and offices may not yet be convenient. Chances are, within a few years they will be.

477. Ask your realtor to look at houses on the market that are of similar house size, land size, and price as the new construction you are considering. Ask what range those houses are currently paying for taxes. In many instances, new construction is taxed under its original tax rate as a farm or other earlier use, so it is not a proper reflection of what taxes will be when you move in.

478. Initial offering prices in a new development are often lower than in the final phases of the development. You may want to look for this relative bargain.

479. Make sure the builder is not likely to run into financial problems before completing the development. Owning one of the ten houses completed in a planned three hundred-house development may leave you with a home that loses value and is surrounded by muddy, incomplete streets and utilities.

480. Check each builder's other projects in the area; multiple projects completed are a good sign that the builder is financially sound. You can also check with the Better Business Bureau for complaints against the builder or with town officials to find out about their feelings regarding the builder.

481. Visit local houses completed by the builder. It will give you a good idea of quality and finishing details.

482. In a desirable area, in a hot market, or with a popular builder, don't be surprised if you are put on a wait list. It may take weeks or months to find out if the builder will even consider your offer if the development is especially popular.

483. Talk to owners of your builder's homes. See how happy they are with the house and with the building process, and find out any other positive or negative feelings the owners my have.

484. If you buy early enough in the building process, you may be able to choose various items and finishes in the house such as cabinets, sinks, tiles, and appliances.

485. If you are working with an agent and want him to represent you in negotiating for new construction, check with the builder's office to see if they allow representation by buyer's agents.

486. Unless a new home or condo is near completion, most new construction timetables are rarely met. If you are moving out of one location allow extra time for potential building delays.

487. Ideally, in new construction there will be very little maintenance since everything is brand new. Consider these savings in your monthly budget.

488. Most new homes are more energy efficient than older homes, which means you'll pay less for utilities every month in a comparably sized house.

489. Most new homes come with a builder's warranty. Many areas of the home are covered for years to come—a great cost savings if anything breaks prematurely. Just read the fine print so you know your coverage.

490. Since new construction is ideally in perfect condition, you may be tempted to waive your home inspection. Don't! You want a licensed professional to go through your new home the same way you would want a licensed inspector to look at an older home. This is your opportunity to spot poorly finished work or other potential problems that could be lurking.

491. Most builders require that buyers write an offer on a purchase contract that was drafted by the builder's attorneys. Since they created the contract, many of the clauses are written to benefit their position, not yours. These contracts usually don't provide a contingency for the buyers to complete inspections. If so, negotiate to include an inspection contingency as an addendum to the contract.

492. In a new development, find out the expected completion date for all construction. Your new neighborhood will be filled with construction vehicles, workers, and noises until then. That quiet Saturday morning you envisioned may actually be filled with the sounds of bulldozers and nail guns.

493. If you value mature trees and outdoor privacy, new construction may not be for you. Many new developments are freshly planted with trees, which will take years to mature.

494. Make sure you know exactly what is included in your purchase price. Paved driveways, sidewalks, and landscaping are excluded from purchase in many instances.

495. If you are buying into a development that will have Homeowners Association dues, be careful of the current and projected maintenance fees. In many cases, maintenance fees are artificially low while the development is still under construction. Projected fees are often underestimated. Add another 30 percent to any number you are given.

496. If you are buying new construction, it is just as important to conduct a final walk-through inspection of the house as it is in a "used" house. Check everything including door swings, painting, moldings, landscaping, and garage door openers.

497. The list of problems you compile upon inspection is called a "punch list." It is the list from which the contractor or builder will work to finish or fix any item not yet completed.

The Fixer-Upper

498. If you are fairly handy, a house needing some TLC may be the right thing for you. Cost savings of a fixer-upper and the pride of doing it yourself could be the perfect mix for you.

499. When looking at fixer-uppers, make sure you are not undertaking projects that are more than you can handle yourself or are cost prohibitive in your budget.

500. Consider the amount of time it will take you to make the house "livable" and compare it to your overall timetable. If you need to be out of your current home by April and the repairs will take until July, you'll need to think about options: living in your new home while it's incomplete, renting elsewhere short-term, etc.

501. If you are buying a fixer-upper in a cold climate, consider the impact of winter on your construction plans. Digging and building a new foundation in northern Minnesota in January may be a difficult task.

502. Expect delays. Wrong cabinets will be delivered. Permits will take longer than the town told you they would. Bad weather will delay your roofer. Make sure you pad your end date accordingly.

503. Look at comparable houses in the area that have been remodeled. Do they sell for a price that would cover both your purchase price and remodeling costs? Have your realtor show you the houses in that area currently on the market or printouts of recent sales.

504. If you are willing to make the investment of sweat equity, consider buying the house that all the neighbors hate. Renovations to the ugly duckling may bring it up to the sale price of your more desirable neighbors' homes.

505. When choosing the layout, design, and materials that will go into your remodeled home, make sure the neighborhood can support the price your updated house would ask. Building a $500,000 house in a $150,000 neighborhood may not be the best investment of your money and time.

506. When purchasing a fixer-upper for your personal use, thoroughly investigate the property and develop a very tight estimate including materials, labor, and landscaping that will make the house viable. Add at least another 10 percent to that cost for overruns and problems you will uncover during the renovation. Subtract the price the home would likely sell at once all of the renovations are done; you'll probably need your realtor to do this. The difference should be your approximate purchase price.

507. If you are purchasing a fixer-upper to resell, also include the costs of selling which include realtor commission and closing costs.

508. Expensive jobs such as complete renovation of kitchens or bathrooms usually boost resell price by more than material and labor costs, but always check with a local realtor before going ahead if your plan is to resell.

509. If you plan to resell a fixer-upper, you are generally better off renovating the items people see: floors, siding, kitchen, baths, and landscaping. Fixer-uppers needing mostly cosmetic work such as painting, replacement of carpeting, refinishing of hardwood, and the like are fairly inexpensive and can more than pay for themselves at resell.

510. Bigger expenditures like replacement windows, siding, and new countertops usually pay for themselves, but are somewhat more expensive; so an eye on the budget and potential resell price is a must.

511. What goes up doesn't always keep going up! Make sure your financial expectations are realistic. A strong local real estate market may continue, or may not. Plan for that unexpected dip or flat market!

512. Have a plan. Know exactly what you are getting into. Develop a budget, long range and short-term time lines and key responsibilities. Never invest in a fixer-upper without a plan!

513. Have contingency plans! Have the name and number of a second plumber or electrician handy in case your first choice has the flu for three weeks or simply vanishes. If your lumberyard can't deliver plywood for two weeks, know where else to go locally so that work can continue.

514. Don't forget all those extra costs: closing costs, commissions on reselling or renting a property, permits, and miscellaneous items like garage door openers that add hundreds of dollars to jobs. Include line items for them in your budget.

515. If you are planning to rent or resell the unit you are fixing up, remember that time off the market is money out of your pocket. The extra month it takes for you to finish your rehab or to find a new tenant or buyer is money out of your pocket.

Expansions and Alterations

516. The listing broker, your agent, your family, and your friends may all tell you this is the perfect home or co-op to expand. Co-op boards may allow you to combine two units, but talk to them first. Meet with town officials to find out what zoning regulations they have that may impact your future plans. Better to know that you can't expand before purchasing rather than after.

517. If you are considering combining neighboring co-ops, you may consider not telling the sellers of your plans. The sellers may think you will be willing to pay a higher price since their neighboring unit is worth more to you than any other non-neighboring unit.

518. If local officials tell you that you can expand, get the zoning or associating rules on paper. Pass them to your engineer or architect so she can develop plans that work within the published rules. (If there is any time lapse between purchase and renovations, you'll want to check with the officials if the building rules have been updated.)

519. There aren't just rules about building heights. There are usually rules about set backs from the street and property lines, amount of surface area covered, etc. The rules may seem intrusive, but they also protect you from your future neighbors building a monolith that overshadows your new home!

520. You'll want to have a survey done of your property if you are planning to expand. It is a great tool for the town officials to look at, and you'll want to be aware of any easements on the property that impact your ability to expand. An easement is a predefined piece of your property that is usable by another party for a specific use like a power line or drainage ditch. Sometimes these uses are not visible to the naked eye, but they may keep you from building the family room or pool you had planned.

521. If your potential plans require a variance, include extra time and money for approvals. Variances are licenses to act contrary to the usual zoning rules, and in many instances, require neighbor notification and appearance at zoning committee meeting(s).

522. When you're developing your building plans, always consider resell factors as well as your personal needs. Remember that kitchens and bathrooms are usually good investments. The house should flow well for daily life and entertaining. An awkward flow will make the house more difficult to sell in the future.

523. Your expansion plans should be in keeping with the neighborhood. Even when your neighborhood is ripe for expansion, try to keep your house in the same character as the neighbors'. It's tougher to sell the most expensive house in the neighborhood, or the house that just doesn't fit in.

524. If you have your heart set on a pool, meet with town officials to make sure you can put in a pool and if there are any restrictions on size, depth, or placement.

525. If the current driveway is gravel, don't automatically assume you can pave it once you purchase the property. Many areas regulate the amount of impervious coverage, and if your property is at its limits already, paving the driveway may require a variance. Gravel driveways may already count as impervious coverage. Some municipalities consider them impervious; some don't. Before you solidify your plans, check with your local zoning officials.

526. Even though decks allow water to pass between the slats, don't assume your town doesn't count decks as part of your impervious coverage. Some towns do, and some don't; so ask ahead of time.

527. Even though a house has been built with an exterior door suitable for a patio or deck, you need to check with town or association officials to ensure the construction of a patio or deck will not exceed impervious coverage regulations. Builders sometimes construct the house to maximum coverage not allowing for additional coverage, so check first!

528. Fences are almost always regulated by local ordinances. Height, style, and placement may be addressed by local zoning rules, so check with your town if you hope to fence in the yard. You may need a permit.

529. Most types of easements prohibit fences running through them. If your potential yard has any kind of easement where you hope to build a fence, check with your local zoning official or the easement holder.

530. If you have spotted that perfect small house that will be ideal for your growing family after you add a family room and two bedrooms, make sure you talk to the town's zoning or construction officer before you make your offer. They'll be able to tell you how much you'll be able to enlarge the home, if at all. You don't want to buy that two-bedroom ranch with dreams of expansion if the town says the house is at its maximum size right now. Better to find this out before you make your offer rather than later; so schedule a time now.

531. If you think you may have found the right house for you, ask if the current owner would share their most recent survey with you. If you are interested in fencing the yard, you'll want to check with town officials regarding rules and requirements that may prohibit you from using the fence style you prefer or the exact placement you want. This is especially true on property with any type of easement.

532. It's not just towns or condo associations that set the rules on expansions and alterations. Many single-family homes are part of homeowners associations. All owners must follow the rules set up by the association. Many of these rules govern fence height, style, and placement as well as shed, play sets, and sometimes even landscaping and paint color. Items as mundane as flags, mailboxes, and flowers may be regulated by the town or association. If your future home is part of an association, ask to review these rules to see if they impact some of your future plans. Keep in mind that the association can enforce rules through fines.

533. Look at other houses in the neighborhood. They will generally give you an idea of what is and isn't allowed. Keep in mind that this is not an absolute rule; many homes have been updated or expanded upon prior to the existing rules, so you may not be able to do the same. Always check with the town officials and the association.

534. When you buy a home in a new subdivision your deed may include covenants, conditions, and restrictions (CC&Rs) that regulate property use. As a buyer in the subdivision, you automatically become a member of the association, and you can't opt out!

535. Some homeowners associations are very strict about their enforcement of rules and others are more laid-back. Just remember that either way, in a few years the pendulum can swing in the other direction.

536. Talk to any residents you know in the neighborhood or ask to meet with a board member. You'll want to get a good feeling for the board, the rules, and the enforcement levels before buying, not after!

537. Homeowners associations have several responsibilities besides setting and enforcing rules. Associations collect dues for routine maintenance in common areas such as landscaping traffic medians. Associations can also impose special assessments to finance improvements or repairs to common areas as in drainage basins or tennis courts.

Financing Renovations

538. There are several ways to finance renovations of a fixer-upper. In many cases it is possible to borrow against cash value in a 401(k) retirement plan, life insurance policy, or stock portfolio. Be careful to look for any penalties, and remember the interest paid will not be tax deductible.

539. There are also home equity loans or lines of credit that allow you to borrow against 90 percent of the equity that you will have in the house after the renovation is complete. Talk to your lender before beginning a project and watch the interest rates!

540. Generally, the higher the percentage of your equity you are borrowing against, the higher rate of interest your lender is going to charge.

541. Home equity loans are mortgages and offer the tax benefits of conventional mortgages usually with little or no closing costs. As with a conventional mortgage, you'll receive the entire loan amount at the closing, and have a specified period of time to repay the loan. Home equity loans usually have fixed interest rates, so your monthly payments are the same throughout the life of the loan, making it easy to figure out your monthly budget.

542. Because the home equity loan is usually second in line to your primary mortgage on the house when it comes to the house as collateral, home equity loans usually have a higher interest rate.

543. Home equity lines of credit are also mortgages but work much like credit cards: you can borrow up to a preset credit limit and pay interest only on the amount actually borrowed, not the entire credit limit. The closing costs are usually nominal in comparison to conventional mortgages. The interest rates are flexible, so your monthly payments can vary greatly.

544. As with all FHA loans, FHA 203K mortgages are insured by the FHA (Federal Housing Administration). They are designed to enable the borrower to simultaneously refinance the first mortgage and combine it with the improvement costs into a completely new mortgage. The loan is based on the estimated value of your home after the renovations allowing you to borrow more money than had the loan been based on the current value of the house.

545. A drawback to FHA 203K mortgages is that the loan maximums vary by county and the maximums are usually fairly low.

Is a FSBO Right for You?

Pros

546. What's a "fizz-bo"? A "FSBO"—or "fizz-bo" in real estate language—is a house, condo, or co-op that is for sale by owner.

547. "For sale by owner" properties may seem like a savings to you, but in most instances, both sides think they are the side that will be saving the commission money! Make sure you know what the right price for that house should be.

548. Just because a house is "for sale by owner" doesn't mean a realtor can't show it to you. Ask your realtor to call the owner to see if the owners are willing to pay the realtor's commission. Since the seller is not using a realtor themselves, they are saving that portion of the commission and may be willing to pay your realtor. This way, your realtor can handle all negotiations, home inspection issues, and closing preparations for you instead of you having to do all of that yourself.

549. Why would anyone sell a house on their own? It could be to save money by not paying a commission or because the seller is confident he can handle all of the details needed to sell and close on his house.

550. Look for "for sale by owner" signs in the town or neighborhood you are interested in. The signs usually include the seller's phone number and ideally, some information about the property.

551. Some neighborhoods or buildings don't allow signs on lawns or windows, so you'll want to talk to neighbors or friends in the area to see if they have heard of any sellers in their neighborhood.

552. Local community centers and supermarkets sometimes have areas where sellers can post their homes. Check frequently since houses sell and the postings are sometimes cleared out by the facilities' managers.

553. Websites such as www.fsbo.com and www.forsalebyowner.com are good sources for FSBOs as well.

554. If you are interested in pursuing a FSBO, your first step is to call the owner to arrange to see the home. You'll want to ask the seller about the specifics of the property: number of bedrooms, number of bathrooms, and any other general questions that ensure you are looking at a house that can potentially work for you.

555. Don't be embarrassed to ask about the price and taxes. You are considering entering a business transaction; treat it that way.

556. In many instances, due to lack of up-to-the-minute knowledge of the market, FSBO owners underprice their homes; so there is the potential to get a bargain.

557. Since a FSBO is not listed on the multiple listing system (on a computer), fewer people will know about the property. Ideally this will keep other bidders away.

558. Sometimes private sellers "over share" information that might be helpful in your negotiations. While you may not want to take advantage of the seller, the extra knowledge may be helpful to you.

559. The seller may not use as much paperwork as a realtor-handled transaction, so there is a timesaving for both parties, although that paperwork is meant to protect participants and clarify various points.

560. Often FSBOs don't require as much money for a deposit, so you can hold on to your money much longer.

561. Depending on the contract you use, buying a FSBO may give you more options to back out of the deal. Make sure you read your contract thoroughly!

562. Depending where a FSBO owner is heading after the move, the closing date may be more flexible.

563. FSBO owners are sometimes more likely to accept a selling contingency from buyers. This could work in your favor.

Cons

564. Keep in mind that FSBO websites tend to be out of date. Unlike local MLS sites, these websites are not updated automatically and sometimes include homes that have already been sold or have since been listed with a realtor. The website managers may update the information often, but sellers aren't always proactive in providing the latest information.

565. For safety's sake, before entering a FSBO, bring a friend, spouse, or family member. You would never enter a stranger's home alone in any other situation, why should housebuying be any different? Remember to tell somebody who is not joining you where you are going and when to expect you back. Carry your cell phone.

536. FSBO sellers are usually in the house, condo, or co-op while you are looking through it. You generally don't have the privacy or time you would like to view the property thoroughly, or take note of the chartreuse wallpaper and matching bathroom fixtures, that you would if the homeowner was not present. You may not feel comfortable inspecting every closet if the homeowner is just steps behind you.

537. FSBO homes can only be shown when the seller is home. If the seller is away for the weekend, at work, or on vacation, the house cannot generally be shown.

568. If you decide to make an offer on a FSBO, do it on paper, and insist that the acceptance also be committed on paper. Verbal agreements give you no proof of contract.

569. Remember to negotiate more than price when dealing with a FSBO. Include the address, lot and block, and closing date in your written offer. You do not want any misunderstanding of what you are purchasing, how much you are purchasing it for, and when you expect to purchase it. Include a written list of exactly what appliances, window treatments, light fixtures, or exterior features you expect to be a part of the sale. This list will be invaluable when you close on the deal. Always, always, put it on paper!

570. As with contracts used by real estate companies, include any mortgage, home sale, or inspection contingencies. You don't want to have the seller misunderstand exactly what you are asking for, so include this information in your written offer. It will become an important reference point after the offer has been accepted.

571. One non-monetary thing to consider if you are buying a "for sale by owner" on your own is the emotional cost. You'll be negotiating directly with the homeowner over sticky issues such as the sale price and necessary repairs. Since there is no realtor involved in the transaction, there is no one there to soften the blow to the seller that you are offering $10,000 less than the asking price because you'll be tearing out his or her cherished orange shag carpeting as soon as you move in.

572. Many homeowners who sell on their own think their house is perfect. Negotiating home inspection issues may get tricky, so tread lightly!

573. Don't give the seller deposit money directly. Find an attorney or neutral party to hold the money in trust. If the deal sours, you don't want the seller to have spent your deposit money!

574. Many homeowners selling on their own will not allow you to hire a home inspector, so make sure you know this when you are making your offer. It's a risk, so base your price accordingly.

575. If you agree to waive a professional home inspector, see if you can find a friend or relative who has an expertise in plumbing, electrical etc., or any system you may have concerns with. The seller may be more willing to let a friend come look at the house rather than an inspector. If all else fails, find a friend or relative who is a general building contractor. They may be able to give you the best advice in lieu of an inspection.

576. If the homeowner will not allow a home inspection or negotiate on any repairs, ask the seller if he will pay for a home warranty policy available from many insurance companies. If you are considering a FSBO house that you fear may need some sizable repairs to major systems or appliances, consider contacting an insurance company that offers home warranties. The policy may cover repairs to such areas of the house.

577. If you are working without a realtor, ask a friend or relative who is a realtor in the area to come look at the potential property with you for a pricing opinion. They may tell you that you are getting a bargain, or they may tell you the opposite; so shop wisely.

578. If a homeowner is persistent enough to sell his home on his own, in the face of dozens of realtors calling to offer representation, he may be equally persistent in his refusal to negotiate or make home repairs.

579. Realtors do not just find houses for buyers. They also coordinate things such as fire inspections and permit inspections, keep on top of deposit schedules, monitor mortgage deadlines, and schedule appraisals. In the absence of a realtor on either side of the transaction, these issues will need to be coordinated by the individual buyers and sellers.

580. Even in regions where buyers and sellers do not normally use attorneys for closings, you should seriously consider hiring a lawyer to review any paperwork and to ensure that proper disclosure is made by the seller.

581. Your local real estate attorney may also be able to provide a template contract for you to use when purchasing from a FSBO. Ask ahead of time.

Landmark or Historic Status

582. The National Register of Historic Places, which is administered by the National Park Service, designates houses that are at least fifty years old and a good example of period architecture as "historic." A historic designation does not restrict the owners from making changes to the property, but it may offer some prestige at resell and add a little to the sale price.

583. Many state and towns offer income tax or property tax reductions on homes with historic designations. These savings may help pay for renovations or upkeep, so keep them in mind.

584. To encourage the purchase and restoration of historic homes, some states permit towns to tax historic homes at pre-rehabbed levels even after they have been restored.

585. States or towns can also designate houses or neighborhoods as historic; these designations are usually stricter than at the national level, so find out what the designation is on the house you are considering.

586. Local designations can be strict and require approval of any cosmetic change seen from the street including paint, doors, windows, and even porch lights. While a local historic designation may prevent you from making exterior changes without approval, it also helps prevent a new, ungainly house from being built next door.

587. Areas not seen from the street, including the back façade and the interior, are usually exempt from any restrictions; but always check first!

588. Once you own a home that that is on the National Register of Historic Places, you can grant a preservation easement to your local preservation society. The easement will protect the structure or façade, whichever you grant, and the easement becomes part of the deed, passing to all future owners. The easement will preserve the façade or structure, and also count as a charitable contribution on your federal taxes.

589. The easement, which in essence is passing your rights to the façade or structure to the preservation society of your choice, will decrease your home's appraised value in turn, reducing your property taxes.

590. A restrictive easement is likely to decrease the interest of future buyers, so it will be a resell consideration when the time comes.

591. Go to www.cr.nps.gov/nr/listing.htm for information on National Register of Historic Places and www.cr.nps.gov/hps/tps/tax/easement.htm for information on historic easements.

4.

Closing in On the One

Finding that special home involves a variety of considerations and a whole lot of time and effort. In all likelihood, you'll visit a house a second and maybe even a third time before making your decision, and each trip back is going to be a little different from the others. Get tips on what to bring with you and what you should be looking for if you're a serious buyer. Learn how timing can play a critical role in whether or not you buy the house of your dreams and get a better understanding of what it means to be in a "hot market." This is also the time to consider the resale value of the house. All of this information will be critical to your next step: making the offer.

592. Always bring a pad of paper and pen for taking notes.

593. Always bring a printed version of your wish list. Keep a log of each dwelling you see and how its amenities match your list. You'll be happy a few days (or even hours!) later when you are trying to keep everything you've seen straight.

594. Stay organized. Consider stapling the listing sheets your agent has provided into a logbook where you can keep notes. This will enable you to reference all of the information at once. (See page 370 for logbook sample.)

595. A tape measure will be handy for checking ceiling heights and making sure your furniture will fit. An electronic version is much faster and convenient to use, but costs more.

596. If you are a little more high-tech, bring along your digital camera, camera phone or PDA for note taking and photographs. Be sure to label your photos. After seeing a few properties, you'll be confused about which bathroom went with which property.

597. Don't forget your cell phone and phone book. You may need to call in a key friend or family member if you think you've found your dream house.

598. You'll need your strength (and blood sugar!) when looking. Pack some portable snacks and beverages along!

599. If you are traveling by car, arrange ahead of time whether you or your agent will be driving. This way you're not embarrassed when the realtor jumps into your back seat that is full of dirty laundry meant for the laundromat.

600. If you are following your realtor in a separate car, make sure you get explicit directions and property addresses. There is nothing worse than being separated in traffic and not having a clue where you should be heading.

601. Ask your agent for area maps or buy your own. You'll want to plan your route the night before to get an idea of the area that you'll be seeing, and the maps will be a great help should you get lost.

602. Maps are also great references for determining distances of prospective houses to shopping, mass transit, schools, highways, and other key destinations.

603. You may want to ride with your realtor; she is not only showing you homes, but during those quiet minutes between houses, she may point out features around town that you may not know about. It's also a good time to see if your personality works well with your realtor's and to really pick their brain about the town, the buying process, etc.

604. Know your limits. See only as many properties in one day as you can handle—usually a maximum of five to seven depending on how far apart they are. Any more than that, and you may not be able to keep them straight (or have the patience to keep looking).

605. Ask your realtor if there is a number where you can leave a message twenty-four hours a day without disturbing them. The home search may be an emotional one and that perfect house you spot at 3:00 a.m. on the way home from the airport may not be available much longer.

606. If you have children, you are usually better off leaving them behind (with a sitter, of course!). It may be tempting to bring the kids so they can "pick out their room" but they'll slow you down, and their shorter attention spans may shorten your search that day.

607. If you must bring your kids along, make sure your car seat is easily transferable to your realtor's car, if you arranged for her to drive.

608. Bring small toys for the kids. They can be lifesavers when you are looking at your fifth house of the day.

609. Your agent should be able to provide school reports for the area you are searching. You can check such sites as greatschools.net for similar information regarding test scores and rankings.

610. If you have a tough time picturing your Scandinavian furniture in the country-cutesy carriage house you are considering, bring along several home improvement magazines or decorating books with before and after photos.

611. Bring photos or measurements of some of your larger furniture with you while you are looking at houses. You'll want to know if your king-sized bed, armoire, media center, dining room table for twelve, and sectional couch can fit into the space available in your new home.

Timing Is Key

312. In a competitive market, try to look for a house when nobody else is looking. One of the slowest times in real estate is between Thanksgiving and New Year's. If you find your dream home during that period, you may have very little competition, and decrease the likelihood of multiple offers. You may even find a seller happy to receive a slightly lower offer price than they would get at other times of the year.

313. Holiday weekends are also great times to beat the crowds and sneak that offer in. Memorial Day, Independence Day, and Labor Day, for example, are when other buyers are busy on leisure activities.

614. If you are buying in a primarily winter-oriented area or summer-oriented region, begin your search just after the last season ended. You may have fewer buyers to compete with and can avoid the pre-season build-up in pricing and competition.

615. In many areas of the country, more houses go on the market just after the New Year and just after Labor Day. You'll have more properties to pick from, but you'll run into more buyers too!

616. You may have other timing in mind. School starts around Labor Day, so in order to close in time for the new school year, you'll probably need to make an offer at least sixty days prior to your intended close date (in most parts of the country). You'll want to start looking earlier than that to allow time for the search itself.

617. Find out the deadlines for your kids' new school before you make an offer. You can try to arrange a closing date based on that date or at the very least, find out the necessary paperwork for enrolling and if exceptions can be made.

618. If you currently have kids in school, check with their school to see if they can finish the school year there even if you move before the end of the year. Many school systems allow students to complete the year if you have moved after a specific date. Find out before you make that offer!

Seasonal Considerations

619. In most areas, trees lose foliage in winter. If you are looking at houses in another season, make sure you peek around those trees to see what your potential winter view will be. That large oak may block a gas station sign nine months of the year. It's up to you if you care about the other three months.

620. If you're moving into an area that is hot or humid in the summer months, chances are you'll want some kind of air conditioning. If the property you are looking at does not include air conditioning, remember that future cost when you making your offer in January!

621. Keep an eye out for low spots, slopes, and other anomalies in the yard that may be a runoff problem in heavy winter or spring rains. When you are looking at the house on a hot, dry August day, you may not worry about it, but that gully directly behind your house may become a torrent with spring runoff in April.

622. Shingles on roofs covered by snow are difficult to inspect. Make a contractual provision to allow you to conduct a second inspection after the snow has melted. You'll want to avoid buying a house without the chance to look at the condition of the roof.

623. In a "hot" market where prices are escalating quickly and the supply of houses can't keep up with the demand, you'll want to ask your realtor to search listings for you every day. Instruct them to call you as soon as a match comes on the market. You may be able to sneak out during lunch, or immediately after work to see it. Sometimes hot properties don't last to the first weekend; so try to get in first.

624. You may even consider putting an offer on a property that you've never seen. If you've really zeroed in on a specific town, condo, or building, and something meeting your needs comes on the market, it is not unheard of to offer on the property sight-unseen.

625. Of course, even in the hottest of markets you'll want to know ahead of time what your options are to back-out of any offer should you have buyer's remorse.

626. In a hot market, houses may receive several offers within hours or days. One way to beat out the competition is to add a phrase to your written offer "We are willing to pay $2,000 above any other written offer up to a total sale price of $300,000." If the sellers accept your offer, make sure your realtor gets copies of the other offers to ensure there really were other written offers!

627. Another way to have your offer accepted instead of your competition's is to make your offer price just over asking price. If the asking price is $150,000, considering offering $151,000. That extra $1,000 may be enough to edge out your competitors who thought offering the asking price would be enough.

628. Write a short letter about yourself and what you specifically love about the house, neighborhood, or area that you are bidding on. Compliments always help, so if you love the new granite kitchen or the current décor, say so. Sellers may want to sell to a buyer who reminds them of themselves or whom they feel will most "take care of their house." Ask your realtor to include the letter with your offer.

629. Although it's usually easier and less awkward to view a home when the sellers are not there, you may want to consider scheduling a follow up visit for a time that the sellers will be home. It may be a great time to ask questions, and more importantly, to bond with the sellers. If they view you as people versus just the numbers in your offer, perhaps they will be less likely to reject your offer or let another buyer outbid you.

630. Ask your realtor to mail letters or make calls to a specific area you are most interested in. She should tell owners in that area that she is working with pre-qualified buyers who specifically asked about their house, street, or building. This may be a great way to find a property that's about to go on the market, but nobody else knows about!

631. You may want to consider making phone calls to the same addresses you asked your realtor to mail letters to. Your follow up call will make the letter more believable and more serious than without the call. You may even bond with the homeowner, which may come in handy during negotiations.

632. Due to federal and state "Do Not Call" lists, your realtor may not be able to call homeowners in an area that interests you, but you can call since you do not represent a business or an organization soliciting business.

633. Go to open houses in the neighborhood you are most interested in, even if the properties shown don't meet your needs. Ask the agent holding the open house if they know of any properties meeting your needs that may be coming on the market soon. The agent may know of something or a neighbor passing through may chime in with some inside info.

634. Keep your feelers out. Mention to as many people as you can that you are looking for a certain kind of property in a specific area. You never know when somebody's neighbor's friend's aunt may be selling the perfect house for you!

635. After making an offer in a very competitive market, don't be surprised if the sellers come back with a request for your final and best offer. If they do, take the sellers seriously, and come back with the best offer for that specific house; consider your very highest price for that house as well as whatever terms and contingencies you can improve in light of any competition.

636. When there are multiple offers on a hot property, ask how many offers are under consideration and if there are any specific areas where the other buyers are beating you out. While the selling agent doesn't have to tell your agent, ask anyway.

637. Agents on both sides of the deal are not allowed to share the exact bidding information of competitors, but the selling agent may speak in vague or general terms. For example, the listing agent may indicate that there are some offers "well over" asking price.

638. Although the listing agent may be inflating some of the information in order to solicit even higher bids, seriously consider the listing agent sharing with you. The information could be a roadmap to presenting your best offer.

639. Consider leaving the closing date up to the seller. By allowing the seller to choose, you may be meeting her most important term. Consider writing the closing as "flexible" or "flexible from March 1–April 15."

640. In a competitive market, you'll be tempted to accelerate many of your contingency dates. Make sure your home inspector, mortgage company, and title company can meet the dates you are offering. The seller will hold you to those dates!

641. Try to see a property before the first open house, and if it's the right house make your offer before the open house as well.

642. For a house that has been on the market for a few weeks, try to make your offer at least a day or two before the open house; you'll want to minimize the sellers' temptation to hold the open house anyway.

643. If your offer is accepted, negotiate that the sellers will cancel any future open houses and will stop showing the house. You'll want get the house off the market as quickly as you can!

644. Surprisingly, open houses don't sell that many houses; so don't panic if the sellers choose to hold the open house even after you put an offer on it. Depending on the market, chances are fairly small that another buyer will make a bid if their first time seeing the house is at the open house.

645. In a hot market, it is even more important to have a selection of comparable properties for each property you are looking at. If you want to make an offer on-sight, you'll want to already know what comps are selling for. Ask your realtor to bring comps to every showing so you can offer an educated price as quickly as you can.

646. Consider including a home inspection as a "for information only" clause. You are basically agreeing to buy the house as is, but at least you know what you are buying. In a hot market, this may separate you from the other offers.

647. In very hot markets, you may have already built equity in the house on the day you close. Your accepted offer in May may be below market value by the time you close in August!

648. If you can afford to put more than 20 percent of the purchase price in down payments, contemplate doing so. Generally, the more money down, the less the home needs to appraise for. This alleviates the seller from any concern about the appraisal, making your offer stronger than other buyers'.

649. In many areas, buyers typically place a small "good-faith" down payment along with their initial offer. To help separate you from the pack, consider a more sizeable good faith down payment. It just may help make the difference!

650. The sooner you schedule your follow up deposits may also give you an advantage. If you agree to place your deposits days or weeks ahead of your competitors, you may be a stronger buyer. Sellers may view you as more serious or more locked into the deal.

When You Think You've Found It

351. Always check into issues that concern you yourself. Your real estate agent is a good initial resource, but always double check the information they are giving you. There are dishonest real estate agents just as there are dishonest representatives in any field. Agents are simply real estate agents; check with experts in each field of expertise that concerns you for the correct and most up-to-date answers available.

352. If you are coming from a small apartment or house, or moving from an expensive area to a less expensive area, don't buy the first house you see just because it is better than where you live now. If the first house is indicative of the new area, there may be even nicer homes in your price range.

653. If you are looking for a quiet street, make sure the street you buy on is not used as a shortcut between two busier streets.

654. You may want to avoid a house on a corner lot, as they tend to have more street traffic and are not as safe for children. The middle of the block and cul-de-sacs are quieter locations.

655. Consider the lot size and shape. Most lots are rectangular in shape. Does the odd lot shape benefit you by providing more privacy or a buffer? Or is the odd shape just extra land to maintain and pay taxes on?

656. Septic system capacity is usually based on the number of bedrooms in a house, not the number of bathrooms. Ask for documentation indicating the maximum number of bedrooms the septic is designed for in the house you are considering. If you want to add more bedrooms now or in the future, the cost of expanding the septic system could make your expansion beyond your budget.

657. Areas with public sewer sometimes have a special annual, quarterly, or monthly fee that is billed separately from local taxes. Ask your realtor.

658. Trash removal is not always free. Many towns have per-bag charges or require private haulers. These fees should be included in your monthly budget.

659. Check to see if the town picks up seasonal debris such as underbrush or leaves. If you need to arrange private removal of your fallen leaves in November, there could be sizable cost associated with all those mature trees in your future backyard.

660. Utility costs vary by region. Electricity is expensive in the Northeast but cheaper in other regions. Consider these costs when looking at a house or condo heated by electricity.

661. Oil heating generally requires periodic refilling of your oil tank. Contact local providers for approximate cost and payment schedules.

662. Local oil companies usually have maintenance plans for oil tanks they fill. Consider these plans since repairs to and replacement of oil tanks can be expensive.

663. When considering oil tank maintenance plans, or service contracts provided by other utility companies, look at any other insurance coverage you have through your homeowners policy or independent home protection plan to make sure you are not paying for redundant coverage.

664. Many utility companies offer monthly payments that are averaged throughout the year eliminating spikes in your bills for summer cooling costs and winter heating costs. Consider these options in your monthly budget.

665. If you participate in a monthly average payment plan with one or more of your utilities, ask what month they reassess the average and bill you for any overages. You'll want to make sure these overages aren't invoiced at the same time as your other utility overages or other months when you expect heavy bills from auto insurance, federal taxes, or holiday credit cards.

666. If a home you are considering is currently heated by oil or electricity, has water supplied by a private well, or has a septic system, talk to local utility companies to see if gas, public water, or public sewer is located near enough for hook up and what the associated costs and regulations are. You may want to consider these switches in the future.

667. During your second showing or second trip to a particular house, you'll probably want to spend more time than your initial visit checking out particulars such as the roof, basement, storage space, and other details you may have overlooked.

668. Study as many aspects of your prospective home as you can during your subsequent visits. You'll want to be aware of as many flaws or defects as possible prior to making an offer.

669. Your home inspection will discover any problems you may have overlooked, but it is best to find the obvious flaws prior to making your offer. By the time the home inspection has occurred, you've already negotiated a price.

670. It's always a good idea to ask for copies of the seller's utility bills; try to get an idea of peak season cooling or heating so you can estimate your future costs.

671. Visit the property you are considering at night to see if off-site lighting from local businesses or traffic negatively impacts your future house.

672. That nearby train stop and the local school are convenient, but are all of those commuters, parents, and kids creating havoc in front of your house every workday? Drive by during the week to find out. Similarly, the quaint church and playground on the corner may be a source of crowds and parking problems on weekends or holidays, threatening your quiet balcony with a cacophony of honking horns and screaming children!

673. Think about the type of items you store, and if your potential house or condo has the right kind of storage space to meet your needs. Large walk-in closets are great for clothing and shoes, as well as off-season clothing such as skiwear. But if you have large items such as luggage, holiday decorations, skis, or a kayak, you may need a basement storage room or an attic to meet your storage needs.

674. The neighboring woods, farm, or golf course may add beautiful views and tranquility to the area now, but check with municipal officials for any potential development there in the future.

675. The one-acre lawn looks stunning in spring. Remember somebody will need to mow, rake, and water that lawn throughout the year. It may be your favorite hobby, or a thorn in your side. Consider your feelings about yard maintenance and the costs of a landscaper.

676. If you are considering condominiums or co-ops because you don't want to handle maintenance issues, look at the monthly association or maintenance fees in comparison to what you may reasonably expect to pay to maintain a small single family home. Consider items like lawn care and snow removal.

677. When looking at condos, make sure you look at the garage, parking spot, or basement storage unit that is included in the sale. The agent may tell you that all of the storage areas are about one hundred square feet, but you'll want to see for yourself. Your unit may be the oddity that is larger or smaller!

678. If you are an SUV or minivan driver or think that owning one may be in the near future, look closely at the garage space. Many garages, even those built since the 1990s have a tough time accommodating one or even two large SUVs.

679. Look at the age of the main systems of the house. Depending on climate and usage, hot water heaters last about twelve years, roofs about twenty years, and furnaces about twenty-five years. If you are nearing the end of the life cycle of any of these, you may want to budget your money in anticipation of making that repair or replacement in the near future.

680. It's never too early to think about reselling. You are the buyer right now, but you'll eventually be the seller (the average American moves every seven years). As you are looking through houses to purchase, consider the top characteristics your buyers will be considering: quality schools, newer kitchens and baths, and a well-planned layout.

681. Right now, solid surface counters in the kitchen and bath are the most sought after. They are also relatively easy to switch out, so if you find a kitchen that has nice cabinets but tired counters, consider upgrading at a later date. You may even make money on the resell!

682. A relatively recent trend is for the family room to be adjoining or very close to the kitchen. This layout aids in keeping an eye on the kids and in entertaining, and is a great feature in resale.

383. If you are moderately handy, look for a place that needs a moderate amount of work like painting and replacing carpeting. The property may be asking less than if it was updated, and a little "sweat equity" can help you make your money back.

384. In many areas of the country, hardwood flooring is the most desirable. Find out if that wall-to-wall carpeting is covering hardwood.

385. The same nice view that draws you to a property is going to entice future buyers. If you have the choice of two properties and you can afford to upgrade your view, you may want to seriously consider it.

386. In single-family homes, three or four bedrooms are usually the most popular sizes, but this varies widely by area.

687. When considering resale, look for a single-family home with at least two or two and a half baths. That is the minimum many buyers are looking for, but again, this varies by region and price range.

688. While the current layout of the house may work for you, consider the needs of your future buyer. Today's buyers prefer larger rooms and an open floor plan.

689. A walk-in closet is very desirable for the master bedroom, as is a master bedroom suite (a master bedroom with a bathroom and, ideally, a small sitting area).

690. Garages also add to resale value. Two-car garages are popular, but three-car garages are increasing in popularity.

691. You may have just moved from next to an airport, so that bus depot doesn't seem so bad; but remember, when it comes your turn to sell, it is going to take longer to find a buyer.

692. Does the house or apartment get a lot of sunlight? It will help when it comes time to sell.

693. A lot of buyers won't even look at a house on a busy road; if your budget allows, you may want to avoid them yourself. Alternatively, you may get more house for your money on a busy road, so depending on your interest in resale, keep an open mind!

694. Homes, condos, or buildings that are within walking distance of shopping, schools, or transportation are usually in demand. A "walk to town" or "walk to train" location will free up your travel time and may net you a pretty penny in the future too.

695. Wallpaper and paneling are not big selling points in today's market. Even if you like the current choices, your future buyers may not.

696. Finished basements, especially in townhouses, can be a strong feature for resale. Families love them for office space or a playroom for kids.

697. A walkout basement or one with full daylight windows is an even stronger selling point. Many towns will allow additional bedrooms to be built below grade as long as the windows or doors are large enough to provide an emergency exit.

698. Is feng shui important to you? Look at the structure and shape of the dwelling, the interior design of the building, the positioning of furniture, the decor, and any other characteristics that your interpretation of feng shui would deem important.

5.

Making the Offer...and What Comes Next

You've found what you think is your new home. Congratulations, but you still need to strike a deal. Learn what considerations you should be taking into account when making an offer, how to decide what your price should be, and how to handle a counter-offer or multiple bid situation. Find out what happens once your offer is accepted. A great deal of time is spent in this part on the home inspection—one of the most crucial steps in the homebuying process. Learn why the inspection is so important and what your role is in the process.

699. Prior to making an offer, ask the seller for a copy of any existing survey. The survey will be useful before making your offer because it will indicate easements, fence placement, and property borders. Potential problems from easements should be considered in your offer.

700. All buyers should ask for and thoroughly read the seller's disclosure before writing any offers. The seller's disclosure is a form which allows the seller to disclose any known material latent defects. These defects are seen or unseen problems that could negatively affect the value or enjoyment of the dwelling or property.

701. Many states require seller disclosures. Disclosure of material latent defects prior to purchase protects the buyer from uncovering serious problems after closing. It also protects the seller since it is proof that a problem has been revealed prior to the sale.

702. If a seller checks off the "do not know" box, don't be alarmed. Rather than incorrectly answering a question, the seller may check "do not know" if they simply don't know the answer. Your home inspection should ideally uncover any potential problems.

703. Surprisingly, sellers don't always take the highest offer. They may find other parts of your offer much more important: Do they want to close by a certain date? Do they want to sell their house "as-is" without making any repairs? Do they only want buyers who don't have a "home sale contingency" (meaning you need to have already sold your home to buy theirs)? Before you make your offer, have your realtor find out what issues are important to the seller. You may be able to meet all of their criteria without any inconvenience to you, and the seller may accept a somewhat lower offer price.

704. Know the comps! Ask your agent to supply you with the comparable houses in the town or neighborhood where you are looking. Your offer should take into account the current trend in pricing. If prices are increasing at 6 percent per year in your area, your offer should allow for this increase.

705. Don't wait until the day you find your dream house to ask for comps; know them ahead of time. If you are targeting a specific area and house size, you can have the comps early so that you are not reacting to information at the last minute and making your decision based on emotions rather than logic.

706. Don't forget to take overall condition and location into consideration when looking at comps. Two houses built by the same builder in the same style and size at approximately the same time may differ dramatically in condition. One house may have updated kitchens and baths while the other has the original twenty-year-old amenities.

707. Exact location also comes into play. Virtually identical houses or condos may vary in price based on their location in regards to the street, parking lot, or transportation. Ask your agent to explain the various comps, giving you the pros and cons versus the dwelling you are considering.

708. A key in negotiations is having your realtor present your offer in the most favorable light. Your realtor should be presenting your offer as serious and fair and include as much of a positive spin as possible.

709. Offers are sometimes presented in person to either the seller's realtor or the sellers themselves. This is why it is critical for you to understand exactly how your agent intends to present your offer. You want to ensure that your agent is presenting your offer in the most positive and credible fashion throughout the entire process, not just the first conversation with the selling side.

710. In most instances, the offer is presented on the phone or fax to the seller's agent. Your agent's presentation skills are no less important than if he were presenting the offer in person!

711. Your realtor should also include a short summary of how much you love the house, condo, or co-op you are offering to buy. This helps put a face behind the numbers.

712. Ask your agent to tell you exactly what she plans to tell the selling agent. You should have the right to edit what your agent intends to say.

713. Ask your agent for advice on your offer. You don't want to pay too much for a house, even in a competitive market, but you may only have one chance to present your offer.

714. Buyers correctly assume that their agent benefits with a higher commission if the buyer pays a higher price for a property. This is true, but in most instances the difference between commission paid to the actual agent increases only a few hundred dollars based on your low offer and your high offer.

715. Sometimes buyers are afraid to offer less than asking price. Sellers may have a less-than-asking-price figure in mind, so if your bid meets that price, you may be in luck. It is surprising how long a property may sit on the market because buyers are reluctant to make a low offer.

716. If you are presenting a less-than-asking-price offer, your agent will generally give a brief explanation to the selling agent as to why—repairs need to be made for example or, similar houses in the neighborhood have sold for less than the current asking price. The rationale will help the selling side understand that you are not simply making a low-ball offer, but an offer based on logical reasons.

717. In many markets, if a house has been on the market for four to six weeks and hasn't received an offer, the sellers may consider reducing the asking price. If you are interested in a house in this time period, you may consider an offer that anticipates the price reduction, rather than waiting for the sellers to lower their asking price.

718. Don't assume that if sellers are divorcing or are deceased that a low offer will be accepted due to the duress. Behind the scenes disagreements by participating family members may make it difficult to negotiate a low selling price.

719. Before you offer, have a final price in mind that you are not willing to spend another $1,000 to get. This may help you keep from overbidding when you are in the heat of negotiations.

720. If you are making your purchase with another person, select just one of you as the primary contact for your realtor during negotiations. You'll want to keep communications streamlined and efficient. But supply the secondary person's contact info as well, just in case!

721. Make sure you give your realtor contact information where you are readily accessible so that the negotiations can continue rapidly. You don't want to be beat out by another bidder just because you were not at your home number.

722. Your agent should ask the listing agent when she expects to hear back from the sellers. This will help you plan your response and allow you to sleep better at night if the seller isn't planning to reply until he returns to town on Sunday afternoon.

723. Consider including a term in your offer or counter offer that says your offer expires within twenty-four or forty-eight hours. This tactic is best used if negotiations are dragging on. You may not want to use this tactic on your first offer at the risk of offending the seller.

724. When you make your offer, and follow-up counteroffers, negotiate all of the points of interest to you during this period. Don't come to agreement on all of the terms and go back a few days later to renegotiate one or several of the points. Sellers may become tired of the back and forth and find another buyer.

725. If you are going to be unreachable for a period of time—for instance, you have a meeting or are on a flight—ask your agent to inform the seller's agent. You don't want the seller to think you are playing games by delaying when you are simply on a plane for a business trip.

726. Fully expect that your first offer will be rejected. Rarely does a seller accept the initial price or conditions of a buyer's first offer unless you offer asking price or above.

727. Unless your first offer is close to asking price, don't be insulted if the seller does not counter offer, or only counter offers a tiny percentage. The seller may feel that her asking price is extremely fair. If that is the case, the seller does not have much room to negotiate down and will be unwilling to do so.

728. Small, incremental counter offers by the seller need not be interpreted as a stubbornness. If the seller has a final price in mind that is very close to the asking price, tiny counter offers may be the sellers' way of getting to that price. Ideally, your counter offer will meet her counter offer on the next attempt.

729. Depending on the region, counter offers may be handled verbally, as long as the initial offer and the final accepted offer are on paper. Ask your agent before you start negotiations so you know what to expect and can plan accordingly if written counter offers are required.

730. Depending on a seller's motivation and how fair she thinks her asking price is, the seller will likely counter offer somewhere between the asking price and the buyers' offer.

731. After the first counter offer, you will hear the phrase "split the difference." If the buyer's and seller's counter offers are separated by $10,000, one side may offer to "split the difference" at the midpoint, or $5,000, increasing the buyer's and decreasing the seller's bids by that amount to agree on a price.

732. In extreme cases, agents may reduce their personal commission and assist either the seller or buyer by helping pay the difference between a stalemated buyer and seller. Again, this is rare since this tactic directly impacts the agent's take-home pay.

733. You may be tempted to begin each negotiation with a "low-ball" offer, one that is in excess of 10 percent below asking price. This tactic may work if the property has been on the market for an extraordinary amount of time or the listing is about to expire, but use your discretion. Low-ball offers tend to insult the seller, so even if your counteroffer is much closer to asking price, the low-ball offer may have soured the deal.

734. Try to view all decisions using both logic and emotion. Determine if a problem that arises during your search or negotiations is a large one or a small one. Logic should be used most heavily when the problem is large, but emotion should always be a factor, especially with smaller problems.

735. Remember that the deal is not over once the negotiations are over. You will be working with the sellers for several weeks or more until the transaction closes. Feel free to negotiate as strongly as you feel is necessary, but remember that you may be looking for some cooperation from your seller at a later date. If you have burned bridges, you may not get the cooperation you are looking for.

Getting Past the Co-op Board

736. Co-op boards usually ask for full financial disclosure including documentation proving current and past salary, current and past employment, current and recent savings and investment statements, current credit report, and recent tax returns. Have all these documents ready prior to making your offer.

737. Review the application and application process with your agent. She can help walk you through the process, especially if she has sold units in that co-op before.

738. Complete the entire application—blank spaces are red flags!

739. Be clear and concise. Answer the questions as they are asked; some positive spin may help, but honesty and clarity win the day!

740. Be on time with your paperwork! You are not presenting yourself in the best light if you are late.

741. Pay attention to details! Give the board the exact documents they request. If they are looking for professional recommendations or letters of employment, ensure that these communications are on company letterhead.

742. When you are meeting with the board, take the time to prepare yourself with the materials you are submitting and organize them in a manner that makes quick reference easy for you. You'll want to look buttoned up, not befuddled as you rummage through stacks of paper.

743. The board meeting may be formal or informal in style; ask ahead of time so you know what to expect. You may get stage fright if you unexpectedly walk into a roundtable interview with ten people when you assumed it would just be a one-on-one!

744. Re-familiarize yourself with your employment history, former addresses, and other personal information and be able to honestly and concisely explain any gaps or repeated moves professionally or personally.

745. Treat the meeting like a job interview. Arrive on time, dress in professional or business casual attire.

746. As with the paperwork you've sub-mitted, answer each question that is asked. If you are applying with a partner, consider dividing topics into likely categories best suited to each partner's strengths or knowledge.

After the Offer Is Accepted

747. Earnest money, good faith deposit, and initial deposit are all terms for the money that buyers put down with their offers to show that their offers are serious.

748. The deposit structure varies across the country. In general, sellers expect 10 percent of the agreed-to purchase price as a good faith deposit. Deposits may be as low as 5 percent depending on region or sale price.

749. Always keep copies of any deposit checks you write. They will serve as proof that you have at least written the check and they can be faxed to the seller's side to show that the check has been written prior to it clearing in the escrow account.

750. Depending on the region and the buyer's finances, the initial offer may be accompanied by a $1,000 good faith deposit. The balance of the 10 percent deposit may be paid after attorney review or the home inspection.

751. The entire deposit structure and timing should be included in the initial written offer so that both sides know what to expect and when.

752. The good faith deposit is usually held in the seller's broker's trust or escrow account. This too varies by region.

753. You can negotiate who holds the deposit money, even in areas where the seller's side traditionally holds the buyer's deposit money.

754. The buyer is entitled to interest paid on all deposit money at the closing. Forms generally need to be filled out at the time the deposit is made, so ask your agent about the process before making an offer.

755. Remember that the overall short time span of a real estate transaction generally keeps interest earnings low, so you may want to avoid the additional paperwork required to keep the deposit in an interest bearing account.

756. If the buyer backs out of the deal for a legitimate reason included in the contract, the buyer should expect to receive the deposit back. Consult your offer paperwork and talk to your attorney first!

757. If a deal is cancelled, both sides must agree on paper to releasing the deposit funds. Disagreements should be handled through the agents or ideally, though each side's attorneys. Remember, real estate agents cannot release deposit money without the written consent of both parties or their attorneys. Agents can lose their licenses for doing so!

758. Serious disagreement on the disbursement of deposits can usually be mediated by the local or state real estate board.

759. The contingencies in your contract generally spell out what needs to happen and when in order to keep the deal moving towards completion. The contingencies dictate the process or flow your transaction will follow.

760. In areas that typically use attorneys to review or close real estate transactions, attorney review may be a preset number of days or simply the period of time it takes both attorneys to agree to the contract provisions. Ask your agent or attorney what is typical for your area.

761. Usually, both attorneys must physically sign off that the attorney review is complete. Ask for a copy of this document for your records.

762. Home inspection contingencies allow the buyer to both inspect the dwelling and property and negotiate for repairs or credits. The home inspection contingency usually sets deadlines for the inspection itself as well as deadlines for the buyer's requests and the seller's response.

763. Part of the home inspection contingency may include inspections for pests, asbestos, mold, radon, well water, and septic or underground storage tanks. Deadlines for these inspections should be included in the contract, as well as deadlines for the buyer's request for repairs and the seller's response.

764. Some areas include a compliance with building codes contingency to ensure the dwelling is up to current codes.

765. Selling contingencies include a clause indicating that the buyer must sell a piece of owned real estate in order to purchase the property currently being negotiated. In markets where there is strong demand, sellers may routinely refuse selling contingencies and simply wait for another offer without a selling contingency.

766. The primary reason a seller dislikes selling contingencies is because if the buyer's own sale falls through, the seller may have lost his sale since the buyer needs to cancel his offer.

767. The mortgage contingency is the most poplar contingency. Most buyers need to secure a mortgage in order to purchase a property. The contingency allows buyers to back out of a deal if they are not able to secure a mortgage by an agreed upon date.

768. Most mortgage companies need between twenty-one and forty-five days to underwrite a mortgage. Make sure your contingency allows enough time. Ask your mortgage representative for a solid timing estimate prior to making your offer so you know how long your mortgage company will need.

769. In competitive markets, many buyers choose to eliminate the mortgage contingency from their offer. This may make your offer stronger than your competitors.

770. If you are tempted to eliminate your mortgage contingency, remember that you will be expected to purchase the property even if you cannot obtain a mortgage.

771. Make sure you meet all of your contingency dates. Mark all of the contingency dates in your calendar or PDA so you can monitor all of the dates, and feel more in control!

772. Call the appropriate parties several days before each contingency must be met. The reminders can keep the details from falling between the cracks and keep the deal alive!

773. Remarkably, there are even contingencies which allow the buyer time to actually see the property if she has purchased it sight unseen. This may be the case in an especially competitive market or for buyers making offers based on Internet postings. Understandably, this contingency is generally short in time since sellers will not remove their homes from the market for long periods of time to allow a buyer extra time to come view it.

Attorney Review

774. In some regions of the country attorneys are used to handle the closing. The agreed-to offer is usually sent to the seller's attorney and buyer's attorney just after the terms are agreed upon. This ensuing period of attorneys rewriting certain portions of the agreement is called attorney review.

Choosing Your Attorney

775. Finding a good, local real estate attorney is a similar process to finding a good, local real estate agent. Ask friends, neighbors, or coworkers if they used an attorney recently for a real estate transaction.

776. Your agent may not legally be allowed to recommend a single attorney, but he might be able to give a short list of local real estate attorneys that have a good reputation in the area.

777. When selecting an attorney, call ahead for prices and services covered for that price. You'll probably want to make your decision based on those criteria as well as how easily you were able to contact the attorney and if you felt confident in her abilities.

778. Ask your attorney about how many real estate closings she handles each year. You'll want an attorney who is active in local transactions but not too busy to work on your deal. Ask if you'll have access to the attorney herself or if almost all communication will happen via the paralegal.

779. Meet the paralegal, if that is whom you will be working with most. A great attorney may be wasted if his or her paralegal is less than competent.

780. Avoid using the same attorney as your seller. You'll want to avoid any potential conflict of interest.

781. You may be tempted to use your uncle Phil, the corporate lawyer, or the your sister, the trial attorney. Strongly consider using an attorney specializing in real estate. He will be better versed in the local real estate laws and processes.

The Process

782. Attorney review is intended as a period for both sides' attorneys to review the contingencies and clauses in the contract and come to an agreement on any modifications. It is not the attorney's job to tell you that you may have overpaid.

783. Attorney review can last a specified amount of time or be open-ended. Ask your attorney or realtor what is typical in your area.

784. Depending on your region and your specific contract, you can typically cancel a deal during the attorney review period without penalty.

785. In states that don't normally include an attorney approval or attorney rider in the contract, you will have to write one if you plan to use an attorney.

786. Don't assume all communications between attorneys are also sent to your real estate agent. The attorneys work for you, not the agents, and may not include them in the correspondence.

787. You'll want to encourage your attorney to do the most diligent job as quickly as possible. In most cases, sellers will not accept additional offers once attorney review is complete, but they may accept stronger offers during attorney review. To prevent competition, a quick attorney review is best!

788. Don't be frightened if attorney correspondence mentions systems such as wells and oil tanks that the property you are purchasing doesn't have. Many attorneys use templates for their correspondence and these templates may include items that don't pertain to your property.

789. Even in areas that do not use attorneys in real estate transaction, you should seriously consider having an attorney review your contract and provide advice. The relatively small amount of money you pay the attorney could save you time, money, and aggravation later, while also making you a more informed buyer.

790. Even if you don't use an attorney, check with town officials prior to closing to ensure that all permits taken for the home you are purchasing are "closed" (meaning all inspections have been handled).

791. You'll want the current owner to attest in writing that to their knowledge, all work requiring a permit did indeed have the appropriate permit. You don't want to close on the house with the possibility that the municipality uncovers work done by prior owners without a permit and you have a fine levied against you.

Home Inspection

792. Buyers can generally cancel a deal after the home inspection if the seller refuses to fix serious problems. Make sure you read your contract carefully and talk to your attorney about the criteria.

793. Do buyers need to be at the home inspection? No, but it is strongly encouraged. It is the perfect time to ask questions about the structure and systems of the house and about any problems that are uncovered.

794. Make sure your inspector reviews all parts of the property including detached garages, basement storage units, and outbuildings such as sheds and barns. Ensure that these are included in your inspection price because you'll want to make sure that these structures are in good shape.

795. Home inspections aren't done just to find the flaws with the house. Inspectors will usually show you important things like how to turn off the water or gas to the entire house or condo and how to flip the circuits in the electrical box. These are small skills you may need in a pinch once you live there!

796. With busy work and personal schedules, buyers are increasingly tempted to arrange home inspections for after-work hours that may lack daylight. You'll want your inspector to see both the interior and exterior in the daylight. Brighter light will make it easier for the inspector to spot flaws.

797. In many states home inspectors must be licensed. Ask to make sure that your inspector is fully licensed. Check americanhomeinspectordirectory.com to see what the regulations are in each state.

798. Excellent resources for home inspection include:

- American Society of Home Inspectors: ashi.org
- National Association of Home Inspectors: nahi.org
- National Association of Certified Home Inspectors: nachi.org
- National Academy of Building Inspection Engineers: nabie.org

799. Not all home inspectors physically go on the roof. Find out ahead of time if yours will. Physically being on the roof generally provides a more reliable, up-close inspection.

800. In states not requiring licenses for inspectors, many have mandatory training or professional associations which have minimum training or service requirements. See if your inspector or inspection company meets these standards.

801. You should receive a written report from your home inspector either at the home inspection or within twenty-four hours. You'll want this report since it will work as a reference tool once you own the house, and just as importantly, it will be independent proof of problems you can negotiate.

802. Your home inspector should be ranking problems in the house along some type of scale from minor to major. This will help prioritize problems for you.

803. Feel free to ask the inspector how important she thinks the problem is. Inspectors have seen many houses, so they can compare the problems to past houses.

804. Although inspectors are not necessary contractors or builders, they may have some idea of the approximate cost of repairs. Feel free to ask your inspector during the inspection. She will probably give you a very lose figure. For a tighter estimate, always contact a contractor.

805. If the home you are buying has a pool, the inspector should examine it while it is full of water and operating. Special attention should be paid to the liner, pumps, filters, and heater.

806. When requesting repairs based on the home inspection report, send along the report with your request to help validate the request and seriousness of the issue. Seeing the assessment on paper from an impartial party (the inspector) could help convince the seller to make the repairs.

807. Do not accept fuse boxes or tube-and-knob electrical boxes! A majority of home insurance companies will not issue fire insurance on a dwelling with fuse boxes or tube-and-knob systems for safety reasons. Chances are great that you'll need to convert to today's standard circuit breaker system before you close.

808. Make all requests for repairs at one time. Don't ask for several repairs one day and several more the next. This could alienate the seller. You may have better luck presenting all of your requests at one time.

809. Keep a copy of the home inspection report in your personal files. It will be a helpful reference tool for repairs that need to be made or problems to monitor once you have purchased the house.

810. Many mortgage lenders require testing for insect infestation—usually wood-boring pests such as termites, carpenter ants, and carpenter bees—prior to lending a mortgage. If this is the case, make sure your inspector covers these points when examining the home, and supplies you with the documentation your lender requires.

811. If you are testing for pest infestation, ask about the cost of this while selecting an inspector because it is sometimes not included in the price you'll be quoted.

812. If you successfully negotiated to have the seller repair any items in the home, ask for a copy of the receipt prior to closing as proof of repair by a professional. This will help ensure a quality, safety-oriented job has been done. If the seller refuses, the buyer should ask to have a home inspector review the repair to ensure it is properly done, or the buyer can inspect the repair during the final walk-through.

813. Keep your home inspection requests reasonable. A good rule of thumb is this: if it is highly likely that the next buyer of the home would want that same item fixed or replaced, you should confidently ask to have it fixed or replaced.

814. Keep the house's age in mind when requesting repairs. Houses settle over the years, and will by definition, have older systems in them. The seller of a 1920s bungalow is not going to upgrade working plumbing just because it is old.

815. Your inspector is only going to be able to assess problems that are visible. Problems hidden by walls, carpeting, or large furniture will be virtually impossible to diagnose.

816. In many instances, sellers who say they will not make any repairs compromise and make some repairs. If the repairs or replacements are reasonable considering the age of the house, the seller may decide to make the repairs to keep the deal alive.

Areas of Interest

Septic System

817. Many areas require that septic systems be inspected by local officials or private inspectors prior to the sale of a home. Find out if the seller or buyer pays for this test and have the agreement on paper prior to the test.

818. A septic system may sound mysterious, but it is made of just a few relatively simple pieces. A pipe removes wastewater from the dwelling into the septic tank. The underground tank, usually between five hundred and twenty-five hundred gallons, has above-ground access for cleaning. Several perforated pipes, usually just two or three feet long, exit the tank and allow liquids to "leach" into the nearby soil; bacteria in the pipes clean the liquid as it passes into the soil which eliminates any impact on ground water.

819. Depending on use, septic systems usually need to be pumped out about every three years. Get the service paperwork from the seller to see the last time the tank has been cleaned. If it is due for a cleaning soon after you close, you'll want to include that cost in your budget. Tank cleaning can cost between $150 and $300 depending on your area and size of tank.

820. When you do pump the tank, ask the service person how full the tank was. This will give you an idea of how often you need to clean your particular tank.

821. The frequency of cleaning depends on the size of your tank (check with your town), and how much liquid and solid waste you generate. Large families, frequent guests, and garbage disposals all add to the load.

822. Don't wait much longer than the recommended time to clean your septic tank— it will cost you more in the long run! If the tank is at capacity, the solid waste will have nowhere to go. The solids may be forced into the leach field, which is designed for liquid waste absorption.

823. A leach field will generally function for about fifteen or twenty years; so check with town officials on the age of your system and if there have been any more recent permits for replacement leach fields.

Pests

824. Your lender may insist that you have your potential home professionally inspected for wood damaging pests such as termites. Even without this requirement, you'll want your qualified home inspector or pest expert to examine the home for evidence of current or past damage and infestation.

825. The U.S. Department of Agriculture estimates that wood-destroying insects of all kinds cause over $9 billion worth of damage each year to American homes. That is more damage on average than all fires, tornadoes, hurricanes, and floods combined in the U.S. each year.

Termites

826. Termites infest millions of homes across the country and the U.S. Department of Agriculture estimates that over $750 million of damages is caused each year from these insects alone. Don't think that because you live in a colder or dryer climate that your area doesn't have termites. Subterranean termites are native to every state except Alaska.

827. Human dwellings make ideal feeding grounds for termites since they provide warmth, moisture, and a food source: wood. Each colony may include up to several million termites.

828. A "swarm" of winged members of the colony is a clear indication that there is a well-developed colony nearby, but even if you don't see this spring phenomenon, it doesn't mean the dwelling is termite-free. The swarm may not have occurred or you may not have been present when it did.

829. Even if you are buying a new home or a home on a concrete slab, your home is not termite-proof. Termites build mud tubes and cross concrete, brick, and pretreated wood to find a food source. Professionally applied treatment is the best way to protect the dwelling.

Carpenter Ants

830. Carpenter ants diminish the structural integrity of a dwelling by hollowing out galleries in the wood.

831. As with termites, carpenter ants search out food, moisture, and shelter and generally enter the dwelling through any access point in the foundation or house. They may drop from overhanging tree branches or utility lines or enter the house on firewood.

832. Professional treatment to the exterior and interior of the dwelling is usually necessary to prevent carpenter ant infestation.

833. If the house you are purchasing has evidence of past or active termite or carpenter ant infestation, you should negotiate with the seller for professional pest control experts to treat the property.

834. If the home inspector suspects termite or carpenter ant damage, you may consider hiring a structural engineer to inspect the structural integrity of the house. Potential structural repairs should be negotiated prior to the sale of the home.

Environmental Concerns

835. When looking at a new property, you'll want to be sure there are no environmental contamination areas that might effect your property or the health of your family. Check with local and state environmental departments for a list of risks in your area.

836. Areas of contamination are often called Superfund sites. These were created by the EPA as a way to identify those places where serious health hazards exist or have existed.

837. To find more information on Superfund sites, go to epa.gov/superfund/sites/locate/index.htm.

Asbestos

838. Look carefully at the insulation in the house you are considering, especially around pipes. Asbestos insulation was used in buildings prior to the 1970s. Asbestos is a mineral fiber that was once commonly used in building construction materials for insulation and for its fire retardant properties.

839. Asbestos is made of microscopic fibers that, when disturbed, may become airborne and be inhaled, causing significant health problems. There is no defined "safe" level of asbestos, but it is known that the greater the exposure to asbestos, the greater the health risk.

840. Asbestos is not always a health hazard; when properly encapsulated, left undisturbed, and well monitored it may be left in the home. Always consult a local professional to determine if there is a potential problem.

841. Tests of linoleum and floor tiles have shown that there is no asbestos danger from the negligible amount of fibers released from even the most worn flooring. Just don't sand or tear these materials.

842. The only way to be sure if insulation contains asbestos is if it happens to be labeled. More than likely, you'll need to have it sampled and analyzed by a qualified professional. Always treat the insulation in question as if it contains asbestos. Sampling should be done by qualified professionals only.

843. If the insulation is damaged, or if your renovations might disturb the asbestos, repair or removal by a professional is needed. It is strongly advised that you hire an asbestos professional.

844. Before hiring contractors or companies to do asbestos removal, ask to see proof of federal or state asbestos training as well as customer references.

845. During asbestos removal, all family members and pets will need to be removed from the home. Make sure you let neighbors know what you are doing and that the company hired will be labeling the area as "hazardous."

846. Before hiring an asbestos removal company, make sure they clearly state how the asbestos will be removed. Before removal begins you should insist that your contractor wet the insulation to help prevent the spread of fibers and dust.

847. It's important to ensure that the area containing the asbestos is taped and sealed to prevent dust from entering the rest of the home. Also, shutting off the air conditioning and heating systems will help prevent the spread of asbestos dust and fibers.

848. Once the asbestos is removed, it is the contractor's responsibility to thoroughly clean the area and ensure that all asbestos dust and fibers are removed.

Radon

849. Radon is a radioactive gas formed by the decay of radium in the ground or groundwater. It is a toxic, odorless gas. While potentially dangerous, high levels of radon can be fixed and reduced.

850. Radon exposure is the second leading cause of lung cancer in the U.S. after smoking, but there is no evidence that children exposed to radon are more likely to develop lung cancer than adults exposed to the same levels.

851. There is no known safe level of radon, so the EPA recommends homeowners with dwellings testing between 2 pCi/L (pico Curies per Liter) and 4 pCi/L be addressed. All homes above 4 pCi/L should be fixed (and many mortgage companies insist that such levels be addressed prior to closing).

852. Before hiring a technician to test your home for radon, contact your state radon office for a list of qualified service providers.

853. Short-term radon testing (two to four days) must be done in closed-house conditions. A small canister which harmlessly and silently measures the amount of radon in the air must be placed on the lowest finished level of the house. The test can be conducted while the house is inhabited; it only requires that for at least twelve hours prior to beginning the test and during the entire test period, all outside windows and doors must remain closed, except for normal entering and exiting.

854. If you come across a home that tests high for radon, start by sealing cracks and other openings in the foundation. Keep in mind, however, that this alone will not significantly lower your radon levels.

855. In most cases of high radon levels, your contractor will need to install a vent pipe or fan. This will not require major structural changes to the home, and it should significantly reduce radon. In many areas the seller traditionally pays for the radon remediation system.

856. If you have concerns about radon or suspect you are buying a home with potentially high radon levels, ask your realtor to include a contingency clause in the real estate contract allowing you to have the home tested and requiring the seller to fix the radon problem should one be found.

857. If a contingency clause isn't possible, consider an escrow account. This will allow you to test the home yourself after the purchase is finalized and use the escrow funds (provided by the seller and held in a separate account) to repair the problem.

Lead Paint

858. Federal law requires that sellers of homes built before 1978 disclose whether or not there is lead paint present in the dwelling as part of the contract. Surprisingly, even sellers who have owned the home since before 1978 often don't know if lead paint exists.

859. Federal law mandates that buyers have up to ten days from the date of contract to check for lead hazards. Buyers or sellers can pay for a lead paint inspection to check for the presence of lead paint.

860. Lead paint may be perfectly safe if it is encapsulated by layers of non-lead paint. Problems tend to arise during renovation. Demolition or sanding may cause lead paint to become airborne.

861. Children under six are especially susceptible to lead paint poisoning. Children's growing bodies absorb lead more readily and their still-developing brains and nervous systems are more susceptible to lead poisoning.

862. Children contract lead poisoning a number of ways, including chewing on molding or windowsills, ingesting paint chips, and being exposed to lead paint dust created by home renovations.

863. Children and adults may ingest lead paint by putting their hands and other objects in their mouths after they have been in contact with lead paint. This includes soil that has been exposed to lead paint, perhaps from the sanding or scraping of exterior paint.

864. Many people think lead poisoning can only affect children. Lead poisoning can cause many problems in adults, including complications during pregnancy, reproductive problems in both men and women, nerve disorders, memory problems, and joint pain.

865. Lead paint poisoning can cause behavioral problems and learning disabilities, or in more extreme cases, seizures and death.

866. Pregnant or nursing women can also pass lead poisoning to their nursing or unborn children.

867. Children who seem healthy can still suffer from lead poisoning. Consult your doctor about testing options.

868. Improper removal of lead paint can actually increase the likelihood of lead exposure! Hire a certified lead specialist for any removal.

869. If you are concerned that your house contains lead paint, have it inspected for the presence of lead paint and also have a risk assessment completed. The risk assessment will tell you how serious the sources of lead paint are in your house and also suggest what actions you should take to remedy the problem.

Mold

870. A good rule of thumb: when there is a moldy smell, chances are good that mold is present! Since mold is caused by water, look for likely sources—around pipes, beneath sinks, or in basements.

871. If you smell mold in a home, but are not able to see it, be sure to ask the seller if he has ever had mold problems and if he has ever repaired mold damage. Find out where the mold was and have your inspector carefully examine the area.

872. Because mold can grow in hidden, moist areas, like behind paneling, under carpets, and behind furniture, a search to uncover a moldy smell might take some time and careful investigation.

873. Inhaling or touching even a small amount of mold can cause potentially dangerous health problems.

874. Reactions to mold can come in the form of cold or allergy-like symptoms—sneezing, runny nose, red eyes, and throat irritation to more serious reactions for asthmatics. Check with your state or local health department or www.epa.gov.

875. To fully eradicate mold from a home, you need to not only remove the mold itself, but you'll need to make sure you eliminate the source of the excess moisture.

876. Be sure to throw away any absorbent materials that have even the slightest mold growth on them like ceiling tiles and carpeting.

877. Removing mold without repairing the cause (the source of the moisture) is an invitation for mold to return.

878. Painting over moldy surfaces, without eradicating the mold, will not solve a mold problem. While it might look better, the problem is likely to return.

879. If you or the seller is cleaning up mold, make sure that the area is fully mold-free and dry before repainting begins.

880. When hiring outside help for mold cleanup, make sure they have enough experience with and knowledge of mold to do the job well.

Well Water

881. Groundwater exists under the surface of the earth in most parts of the country. Private wells access this water for use as drinking and cooking water. Wells are more prevalent in rural areas throughout the country and in areas that were rural in the past fifty years but are now being developed. Homes with wells are sometimes located in the same neighborhoods as houses with public water.

882. Contamination from runoff, oil, pesticides, or various chemicals can affect the quality of the water. Contamination can spread from one property to the next, so the source may not be on your property.

883. Most states require that private well water be tested prior to the sale of a home. Check with your agent and inspector for safe levels and confirm if you or the seller are paying for the inspection.

884. Buyers shouldn't buy a house without inspecting the well. Most states and lenders will require that you do. This is the water you'll be using for drinking, cooking, and bathing.

885. Ask the seller or the company that drilled the well for the well history report, also called the well log or drilling report. Most states require well companies to file a well history report for each new well drilled.

886. Inspect not only the quality of the water, but also the mechanical components of the well and the wellhead.

887. The well history report typically includes the well drill date, location of the well, type of drilling used, type of casing or lining used, well depth, type of screen, and type of pump. All this information will be useful should you need any repairs or maintenance on the well.

888. You'll also want any maintenance records or inspection records the seller may have.

889. Before purchasing, your state, county, or lender may require you to test the well water for total coliform, fecal coliform, nitrates, pH, and volatile organic compounds, which are industrial and fuel-related chemicals.

890. A local well water inspector should know exactly what problems to look for and what levels are considered acceptable, borderline, and excessive. Make sure your inspector knows the local, state, and lender requirements and is licensed to perform the necessary tests.

891. PH levels are important, not only because they may change the look and taste of your water, but because an acid or base level that is too high may damage your pipes, causing unhealthy minerals to leak into your drinking water.

892. Bacteria and chemicals can enter your well water in several ways. Some contaminants such as arsenic and lead occur naturally. Other contaminants stem from human and animal wastes, storm water runoff, and farm runoff.

893. You should continue to test private wells annually for nitrate and coliform bacteria. You'll want to detect any contamination early. Both nitrates and coliform may indicate exposure of well water to human or animal waste.

894. If you have heard of local problems with pesticides or radon, test more frequently.

895. Your local health department and local public water company may be able to supply you with local well water quality in your area and what contaminants you are more likely to find.

896. Wells should be located uphill from any pollution sources such as septic systems.

897. Each state has minimum requirements for distances from pollution sources, generally one hundred feet. Your local health department will have information on the standards.

898. Fine textured soils filter impurities from ground water better than coarser soil types

Exterior Insulation Finish System (EIFS)

899. If you are considering the purchase of a home with exterior synthetic stucco, you may be buying a home with EIFS. Made of foam board, EIFS, or Exterior Insulation Finish System, was designed as a waterproof system for siding homes.

900. When improperly installed, the EIFS waterproofing system actually becomes a big problem. Because it doesn't have a built-in system for water drainage, any water that does penetrate its barrier isn't able to escape and will eventually soak into the wood structure of the home, causing potential problems like mold, rot, carpenter ant or termite infestation, and general wood decay.

901. While carpenter ants can be simple to treat in a traditionally sided home, they are more difficult with EIFS siding. Because the moisture is trapped within the wood, the ants have no reason to migrate to the exterior, making treatment almost impossible.

902. Termites are another common problem with houses sided in EIFS. Because of the nature of the foam panels, it is often difficult for homeowners and inspectors to detect the bugs until it is too late.

903. In many instances, it has been discovered that termites have used the foam panels as a tunnel from the ground to the wood structure, making them difficult to find.

904. The nature of EIFS systems makes them an ideal environment for mold growth. Once the water reaches the void behind the panels, there is no way for it to escape and the often-cool conditions will create mold.

905. EIFS itself should not necessarily be a deterrent to your purchasing decision. Most of the problems created by EIFS are prevented with proper installation and the use of proper flashing materials around windows and doors.

906. When inspecting a home, ask your inspector to carefully examine the areas around door and window openings, and places where EIFS meets other materials like wood trim, stone, brick, or deck connections. Any signs of water penetration could mean you run the risk of some of the problems discussed earlier.

907. Resale values on homes using EIFS are often lower than similar homes without EIFS. Some corporate relocation programs specifically exclude homes clad with EIFS. So be careful when you are thinking about resell.

908. In many areas, there are lawsuits pending against builders who have installed EIFS stucco. Find out before you bid and do research into the litigation so you know what situation you are buying into.

909. If you are buying a property with EIFS stucco, consider asking the seller to hold money in escrow for a predetermined amount of time to allow for future repairs or replacement of the stucco.

Oil Tanks

910. When homeowners first began making the switch from oil heat to natural gas, it was common and acceptable practice to leave the old oil tanks buried in the yard. Not surprisingly, some of these tanks now present potential environmental and safety hazards.

911. There are approximately three to five million oil tanks still buried underground in the U.S. If you are considering buying a home built prior to 1970, it is likely you are buying a home with a buried oil tank.

912. Buying a property with a buried oil tank is not necessarily a bad thing, as long as the homeowner has written documentation that the tank is properly maintained or was abandoned properly according to state and local safety guidelines.

913. Proper methods for abandoning unused oil tanks usually involve pumping out any remaining fuel, cleaning the tank, and filling it with a local- and state-approved filler—often cement or sand. Check your state and local guidelines to find out what is acceptable in your area.

914. Major costs can be involved if an improperly buried oil tank is discovered on your property. Soil and water contamination can cause both health and environmental safety issues and the cost of detection and removal can be a significant expense.

15. Signs that an abandoned oil tank might be improperly buried on the property include: pipes sticking up from the ground near the home or extra fuel lines entering the basement from the outside.

16. If you are buying a home with an aboveground heating oil tank, ask the homeowner for proof that the old tank has either been removed or properly abandoned.

17. Contact the local building inspector if you have any concerns about an oil tank on the property you are purchasing.

18. If you suspect that an oil tank has been improperly abandoned on the property, ask your inspector to carefully look over the property and consider asking the homeowner to bring in an oil tank removal company for a full investigation. If an oil tank was abandoned by previous owners, many sellers will not even be aware of its existence.

Flood Zones

919. If you think you are buying a home with a high risk of flooding, contact FEMA or your community's building office to learn whether or not they participate in the National Flood Insurance Program (NFIP). NFIP is a federal program that allows property owners in participating communities to purchase flood insurance.

920. Nearly twenty thousand communities across the United States and its territories participate in the NFIP, which requires them to follow specific guidelines in an effort to reduce future flood damage. In exchange, the NFIP will make flood insurance available within the community.

921. If your community participates in NFIP, flood insurance is available to every property owner, whether or not you think you are in an area with high flooding potential.

922. If you are buying a home in an NFIP designated flood zone, you will probably be required by your lender to obtain flood insurance whether or not your home is in an area participating in NFIP.

923. The risk of buying a home in a potential floodplain not participating in NFIP means that you will not be able to purchase federally backed flood insurance and might lose out on some federally backed assistance programs.

924. Twenty-five percent of all flood claims occur in those areas designated as low-to-moderate risk. Flooding can be caused by the obvious culprits like rivers, lakes, hurricanes, and tropical storms; but when considering insurance don't forget some of the other most common causes of floods like melting snow, inadequate drainage systems, and failed protective devices such as levees and dams.

925. It is recommended that all property owners purchase and keep flood insurance. It is the best means of recovery from flood damage of any kind and is in your best interest to obtain some.

Electromagnetic Fields

926. The movement of electrical currents generates electromagnetic fields or EMFs. Using any electrical appliance creates an EMF including hair dryers, alarm clocks, and microwaves. As of now, there is no direct link between EMFs and health problems; however, if a house that is close to high-tension wires makes you uncomfortable, you can hire an inspector to measure EMFs. Knowing that the EMF reading is low may help put your mind at ease.

6.

Tying Up Loose Ends

Once the offer has been accepted and your mortgage has cleared, you probably think you can start relaxing. But there are still a number of things you'll want to do before the closing and final walk-through. Now is the time to think about scheduling any repairs you feel need to be done and bringing in decorators for any work you would like completed before you move in (but not before the closing). While you won't get the decorators working yet, you can show them the house so they can prepare a plan.

927. If your schedule and finances allow for it, consider a quick close that meets your seller's needs and also allows you time to make the repairs you need prior to moving in. Stay in your old apartment or house for a couple of days or weeks while you paint or refinish the floors.

928. It is easy to make repairs while the house is empty. Professionals will sometimes charge you a less expensive rate if the new property is vacant.

929. If you have time between moving out of your old house and moving into your new one, you can schedule repairs to your plumbing, electrical, or heating and cooling systems while the house is empty. The dirt stirred up by those messy jobs may make a mess of your new comforter or couch, so avoid scheduling this work after your move.

930. If you have a series of repairs to make, ask each repair team where in the list of repairs their work should fall. You don't want the painter's work undone by the central air conditioning installer drilling holes in your ceilings.

931. Repairs typically go over budget. One repair uncovers another necessary repair. Replacing windows may uncover termite damaged framing. Have an emergency fund for hidden problems.

932. Certain repairs prompt you to make other repairs at the same time—replacing the kitchen counters may require you to replace the backsplash or sink. Pad your budget to anticipate the unexpected.

933. An overlap also allows you to move in more slowly; perhaps you can drop off a car full of boxes each day on your way home from work. It makes a big move seem less daunting.

934. Get a list of local utility providers from your realtor so that you can change the billing information to your name starting the date of the closing. Some providers require a week or two notice to process the request, so make those calls ahead of time.

935. Many utility providers have websites that enable you to adjust billing information online; it might be the quickest way to handle this tedious process. You may even get some money-saving hints from their websites.

The Walk-Through

936. Different states have different rules regarding when you may back out of a deal. Ask your realtor to give you a written copy of the offer paperwork you'll be signing ahead of time. Read through the sections that discuss your options and penalties for canceling the deal; this way you know what your options are throughout the process.

937. Make sure you conduct a walk-through inspection of the home you are buying within twenty-four hours of closing. This will be your last chance to see the house prior to you actually owning it.

938. Bring an extra set of eyes. You will be nervous and excited on the day you close on your house. Bring a friend along who is not part of the transaction to help with the walk-through. An objective person, and ideally, a person that hasn't seen the house before, may notice things you might overlook.

939. Ideally your walk-through will occur after the seller has moved out. You'll be able to see walls and floors formerly blocked by furniture and area rugs.

940. Ask your agent to bring a checklist of appliances and light fixtures that are to be conveyed with the house or condo. With your emotions running high, you don't want to overlook the missing washer and dryer.

941. Check to make sure all of the agreed-to repairs have been made and appear to be done correctly.

942. Look for damage done by movers: gouges in walls, broken windows, and scuffs on flooring. They should be addressed by the seller.

943. Test as many systems as feels comfortable: turn up the heat or air conditioning depending on the season, run sinks, flush toilets, open and close windows. It will be easier to have the seller fix these items if you know they're broken before the closing rather than afterwards.

944. Look in the basement and attic for water or evidence of water damage that was not there during the home inspection. The roof may not have leaked during the January snow, but it may be leaking in the March rains.

945. Most contracts specify that the house must be "broom clean," the grass must be cut, and the snow removed on the day the title transfers to you. If the sellers haven't handled those responsibilities, you can ask for money back at the closing or delay the closing until the chores have been taken care of by the seller.

946. Allow adequate time between the walk-through and the closing to address any issues that have come up. A walk-through ending fifteen minutes prior to the closing will not enable anybody to rectify a problem in time for the closing.

947. It's generally not recommended to hire a home inspector to accompany you on the final walk-through. Ideally you have found all of the serious issues with the house during the initial home inspection and any repairs have been documented with receipts.

948. By the time you do your final walk-through, you have long since passed your contract's home inspection clause. You should be looking for items that have not been repaired and extraordinary deterioration of the property or home since your bid was accepted. Determining that the roof or furnace is thirty years old is not going to help you at this point.

949. If a repair has been completed that is complicated or technical in nature, or if there is simply a repair that concerns you, you can consider asking the home inspector or an expert in that specific field to examine that specific repair at the walk-through, or earlier if possible. Their fees should be much lower than a full-fledged home inspection since you are only asking for the inspection of one component.

7.

The Closing
and Beyond

As the closing date approaches, both your nervousness and your excitement levels will probably increase. Luckily there are still a number of safety nets in case things should go wrong. In this section, you'll learn tips and tricks on asking for or requiring escrow, what to look for during your walk-through, and how to handle the closing.

950. Escrow is a fancy word for a trust account. It's an account where money is held temporarily until certain preset conditions have been met or resolved.

951. Wherever possible, you'll want your attorney or representative to "hold," or be responsible for maintaining, the escrow account. Generally, you'll be in a stronger position if the transaction sours and your side is more in control of the escrow.

952. Because property tax liens take precedence over mortgage liens on a property, lenders usually require that borrowers pay their property taxes through lender monitored escrow accounts. At closing, your lender will generally require you to pay into a real estate tax escrow account, and as your tax bill becomes due, your lender will pay your taxes.

953. Some lenders waive mandatory escrow accounts for property tax payments if the borrower puts more than 30 percent down in cash.

954. Some states require lenders to waive mandatory escrow accounts if borrowers pledge a savings account that contains sufficient funds to pay property taxes. The borrower maintains control of the account. You'll be required to carry a minimum balance to cover the taxes and you are responsible for facilitating the tax payment, not the lender. The minimum balance in the account is usually one year's worth of taxes. The account can be interest bearing.

955. In some states, lenders may charge borrowers a one-time fee for not holding a property tax escrow account. Some states forbid this charge, so check with your attorney about it.

956. Federal law does allow lenders to require escrow accounts for homeowners insurance payments. The insurance protects the lender's investment in your home.

957. Most lenders do not pay interest on escrow accounts, but always ask because it may be available in your state.

958. In many areas it is customary to hold money in escrow for heating or cooling equipment that couldn't be tested off-season. Ask your attorney or agent about this and what amount would be appropriate. Usually when the system is found to be in working order, the escrow money is sent to the seller at a predetermined date.

The Closing

959. The closing or settlement is when the title passes from the seller to the buyer.

960. The closing usually takes place in the buyer's attorney's office or at the buyer's title insurance office. Find out ahead of time so you know where you are headed, especially for a 9:00 a.m. closing!

961. Sellers can usually sign their paperwork ahead of time, so they may not be at the actual closing. Buyers generally have much more paperwork to sign and should make every effort to be at the actual closing. The purchase of a house, condo, or co-op will probably be one of the largest purchases you make and the largest debt you have.

962. If you are having an escrow closing, neither party attends. Documents are completed by the buyer and seller. Money is disbursed by the title company via escrow accounts once all of the paperwork has been properly completed and all instructions have been followed.

963. For closings scheduled at the beginning of the month, the lender will require a prepayment of the interest from the closing day until the end of the month. The earlier in the month you close, the more interest you'll be prepaying.

964. If you are debating a December closing versus a January close, consider the tax implications. Any points you pay at or before closing as well as any prepaid interest will be deductible in the year you paid them. A December close may be more advantageous to you, but check with your tax preparer.

965. Avoid the last week of the month if possible. They are typically the busiest weeks for title companies, financial institutions, and movers. Your attorney or title company may have an overbooked schedule, so reserve your time well in advance.

966. Federal law mandates that lenders supply you with what is called a good faith estimate of closing costs. The document will itemize approximately what costs you will incur at closing. Remember, it is only an estimate, so actual costs may vary.

967. Always read the documents you are signing. Make sure all of your personal information is correct as well as the interest rates, points, and terms of your loan.

968. Ask your attorney or mortgage representative ahead of time how much money you need to bring to the closing and in what form. Most lenders require bank or certified checks, not personal checks. You don't want to scramble around for a bank check in the middle of your close, especially if you are closing after bank hours.

969. Bring your personal checkbook to the close. There may be some last minute payments you need to make and a personal check might be acceptable.

970. You should receive all keys and garage door openers at the closing. If your house, condo, or co-op has a separate key for the mailbox, storage unit, front gate, or lobby, you should receive those as well. It is always a good idea to change the applicable locks after you close for safety concerns.

71. If you haven't already received the condo or co-op rules and regulations, you should receive them at the closing. A gentle reminder to your attorney or realtor a few days before the closing may be helpful.

72. Ask your realtor to get the seller's new address and phone number. If you get to the house and the seller has left something behind or forgotten to give you the back door key, you should ask your realtor to contact the seller for you.

73. If some keys happen to be missing, you may also ask the seller's realtor. He may have a set that he used when showing the property.

74. Title and deed are not the same thing. Title, which passes to the buyer at closing, is the concept of right of ownership. The deed is the physical document that shows who has title to the property.

975. Your deed needs to be recorded. Depending on your area and the type of closings traditionally held there, your title company or your attorney will record the deed with the local recorder of deeds, generally the county courthouse or county government.

976. Recording the deed is public record of your ownership of the property, and in many cases, public record of your purchase price.

977. At the closing, proofread any and all documents, including those pertaining to the deed. You'll want to ensure that the correct name(s) are on the deed, as well as any addresses and lender information. An incorrectly filed deed may disrupt property tax billing. You do not want property taxes to go unpaid!

978. Did the sellers promise to include the refrigerator as part of the purchase of the house but instead took it with them? If it suits both parties, you can negotiate a credit for the purchase price of a new fridge rather than insisting they move the old one back in. Do a quick Internet search for a similar size and style of refrigerator (and don't forget to include delivery charges!) to come up with a credit amount that is fair to you and to the forgetful sellers.

979. If items were not repaired properly per your agreement after the home inspection, you can ask for a credit to cover the repair or correction. Consider calling a repairperson for a quick quote to get an idea of an appropriate amount.

980. If a closing needs to be cancelled or rescheduled because of problems uncovered during the walk-through, weigh the benefits and risks of scheduling another day or half day off from work rather than closing on a house not in the proper condition.

981. If unexpected scheduling conflicts arise last minute—a death in the family or an unavoidable business trip—try to give all parties as much advanced notice to reschedule the closing. Because the seller is trying to relieve himself of the financial burden of the house he is selling, chances are he will be happier to move the closing forward rather than back. Try to keep your options open for a new closing date in either direction.

982. If you absolutely cannot get to the closing, you can assign the power of attorney to another person, meaning they can legally sign documents for you. You'll generally want to limit the power of attorney to one day and this one transaction. Your real estate attorney is probably your best choice.

83. Try to keep things in perspective. Generally, the seller is not out to intentionally hurt you. If items are damaged or missing, it is most often purely an oversight or misunderstanding.

84. Try not to be accusatory. Be solution oriented. Work to resolve whatever problems arise.

85. Believe it or not, you may be in the driver's seat. Before you panic, remember that generally, as much as you want to close the deal, so do the sellers. They may need the money from the house you are buying for their next purchase.

86. If the seller hasn't moved out by the scheduled closing time, do not close! Talk to your agent and your attorney immediately.

987. If the seller has yet to move out, you can consider closing but charging the seller rent until a pre-agreed-upon date. You'll want to have the new move-out date and all details of the rental agreement on paper so you have a full understanding of what is happening.

988. Your attorney can give you a good idea of what kind of daily rent to charge. She can calculate the fees and payments you'll owe for mortgages, taxes, and out-of-pocket costs during the rental period.

989. Remember utility costs, insurance coverage, and any cancellation charges you incur due to the delay can be passed to the seller; but you must have agreement ahead of time.

990. Remember to schedule a new walk-through prior to your rescheduled closing! A vindictive or careless seller may have caused damage since your last walk-through inspection.

991. Sometimes problems that delay the closing are not actually caused by the buyer or the seller! If a horrible storm hits your region, your closing may have to be delayed. Watch local weather reports a few days prior to the closing. If you anticipate disruptive weather on the scheduled closing date, see if you can arrange a new date, ideally before the bad weather, to avoid any delays.

992. If you predict a delayed closing, have a contingency plan worked out ahead of time. Your plan should include housing during the delay, rescheduling of the move, arranging for utilities and a locksmith, and notifying your lender and insurer.

993. Unfortunately, lenders don't always wire the money needed for the closing in time or in the correct account. A reminder call to your lender or attorney a few days before the scheduled closing can't hurt.

994. Loan packages from lenders sometimes do not arrive in time for the scheduled closing. If they are arriving from out of state, you may, unfortunately, have to wait until the next day's overnight delivery. If the package, or missing documents are coming a shorter distance, insist that they be messengered to your closing location at the lender's cost, of course!

995. You should have already had a title search completed on your property. Occasionally, title problems arise at the last minute. Recent property taxes may not have been paid, or a contractor may have filed a lien against the property due to lack of payment. Don't close until you have spoken to your attorney or your title company.

996. Unfortunately, buyers and sellers occasionally die prior to the closing date. If they seller dies after signing the contract, the estate is generally obligated to complete the transaction. There may be a delay while details are being handled. If you, your spouse, or your partner dies, you may not be obligated to complete the transaction. Read the contract and contact your attorney.

997. If there are serious physical problems with the dwelling you purchase after the closing that were not disclosed by the seller prior to the sale that are not the result of normal wear and tear and should have been known by the seller, contact your attorney.

998. Your attorney may suggest that you have a licensed home inspector or certified professional in the specific field of your problem visit the dwelling and write a report based on the findings. The report should document the cause and symptom of the problem as well as the likelihood that the previous owner should have known about the problem. That report should be sent to your attorney.

999. You may first choose to send the home inspector's report to both real estate agents and the seller to see if the seller will agree to compensate the buyer for any and all repairs. This is the ideal resolution.

1000. If legal action becomes necessary, your attorney will generally file a claim against the seller, as well as both real estate agents and the companies they represent. This is done to prevent the one or two named parties from simply blaming the one unnamed party for the problem.

Glossary

Abstract of Title Usually found in your town's records hall, this is a summary of all legal proceedings including liens against the property, unpaid taxes, and other financial difficulties on the title of a property.

Acre a measurement of land equal to 43,560 square feet

Addendum any addition or modification made to a contract

Adjustable Rate Mortgage (ARM) loan with an interest rate that is periodically adjusted to reflect changes in the prevailing interest rate

Agent a person licensed to represent a buyer or a seller in a real estate transaction. Unless they are also brokers, agents must work in association with a real estate broker or brokerage company. *Also Real Estate Agent

Air Rights rights extending from the surface of the earth towards space

Allergens anything that can cause allergic reactions, most commonly pollen, pet dander, or dust

Appraisal process of determining the value of a building, usually by comparing one structure—home, apartment, or condo—to similar structures in the immediate neighborhood

Appraised Value appraiser's opinion of the current market value of a property

Arts-and-Crafts Style a design style usually defined by its fine craftsmanship, use of woods and metals, simple, clean lines, and masculine look

Asbestos a mineral fiber once commonly used in building construction for its fire-retardant and heat-resistant characteristics that is known to cause health problems and certain cancers if inhaled

As-Is Condition selling or purchasing a property in it's existing condition, with no modifications or repairs

Asking Price the price a seller is asking for the home

Assessed Value used to calculate taxes. It's the tax assessor's determination of the value of a home.

Assessment the estimated value of a home

Assumable Financing mortgage that can be transferred to another borrower

Backup Offer secondary bid accepted by the seller if the first offer falls through

Bonus Room a room with no specific function, unlike a living room, bedroom, or kitchen

Bridge Loan short-term loan for borrowers who need more time to find permanent financing

Broker a licensing designation that allows someone to handle property transactions and operate a brokerage firm

Bungalow a small one-story house or cottage that's built low to the ground and has a low-pitched roof

Buyer's Agent a real estate agent representing a buyer in a home purchase

Buyer's Market a market condition that favors the buyer—usually this means there are too many homes for sale and a home can be bought for less than asking price

CC&R The covenants, conditions and restrictions (CC&Rs) are the governing legal documents that set up the guidelines for the operation of the planned community as a non-profit corporation. The CC&Rs are recorded at the local County recorder's office and are included in the title of the property. Failure to abide by the CC&Rs may result in a fine to a homeowner by the Association.

Cape Cod style a traditionally wood-frame or shingled house (although many might now have steel or aluminum siding) with a steep roof and several windows or dormers projecting from the second floor

Capital Improvement an improvement that is going to increase the value of the property. Such improvements may include a new roof, central air conditioning, new windows, an addition, or a garage.

Closing the day when all papers are signed to officially transfer ownership of the home and finalize the sale

Closing Costs expenses paid by the buyer and seller when the deal closes. They might include brokerage and agent commissions, mortgage fees, escrow, attorney fees, transfer taxes, and title insurance.

Commission payment received by real estate brokers and agents for their work on the sale of a property

Common Area the area in a building that is shared by all of the tenants and owners of the building, including lobbies, courtyards, hallways, and gardens

Comparative Market Analysis (CMA) a report showing prices of comparable homes that were recently sold in the same area, also called competitive market analysis

Competitive Market Analysis (CMA) See comparative market analysis

Condominium a form of ownership in which residents have ownership of their individual units in a building or development

Contingency a contractual provision establishing conditions that must be met prior to closing. This might include repairs, financing, or attorney approval.

Co-op a building or development owned by a corporation in which shareholders live in the building and lease specific units

Counter offer a response to a bid with a new price offering

Craftsman Style an architectural style that evolved as part of the Arts and Crafts movement near the turn of the 20th century

Credit Report a detailed account of an individual's credit, employment, and residence history. It's used by lenders to determine loan amounts, interest rates, and terms.

Cul-De-Sac a street or alley that is closed at one end

Deed the document used to transfer property from one owner to another

Deposit money paid by the buyer at the time the contract is signed to show good faith that he intends to follow through with the deal

Down Payment Unborrowed cash put into the purchase by the buyer

Dual Agency when one real estate broker represents both the buyer and seller

Duplex Apartment an apartment that has an upstairs and downstairs level

Dutch Colonial Style a barn-like home with a gambrel roof, a ground-level front porch, and dormers

Easement the right to use the land owned by another person, most often your neighbor or utility company

En Suite Bathroom a bathroom that is directly connected to an adjoining bedroom

Encroachment when a property owner builds a structure or fence that occupies a neighbor's land

English Tudor Style a home design featuring stone or brick exterior walls and exposed beams

Equity the value of a home after existing loans are deducted

Escrow the procedure of placing money in an account where neither buyer nor seller can access the money without the consent of an escrow agent. Money remains in escrow until both parties conclude that the pre-agreed terms for release have been satisfied.

Façade the front of a building

FSBO a property that is for sale by owner

Federal Housing Administration Loan more appropriately called "FHA Insured Loan," a loan for which the Federal Housing Administration insures the lender against losses the lender may incur from borrower default

Federal Style a style of home, found primarily in the United States, that includes bigger windows and a front doorway surrounded by glass and topped with an arched window

Feng Shui an ancient Chinese system that studies the relationship between people and the environment in which they live. Feng Shui techniques and design are used to maximize harmony between spiritual forces and the influence they have over the spaces where we live and work.

FHA See Federal Housing Administration Loan

Fiduciary Responsibility a legal term for a position of trust and confidence

Fixed Rate a type of mortgage offered by lending institutions in which the interest rate remains constant over the term of the loan

Fixture anything of value that is permanently attached to the property including installed carpeting (not rugs), light fixtures, fences, and landscaping

Floating Rate a type of rate offered by lending institutions in which the interest rate fluctuates with the prevailing rates offered to lending institutions

Florida Rooms enclosed porches built onto a home

Foreclosure when a lending institution takes back the property because the property owner can no longer meet payment agreements

Georgian Style a home style distinguished by its symmetry, a prominent front entrance, and decorative blocks set in the corners of the house

Greek Revival Style like the White House, this style has prominent pillars in front of the house

Half-Bath a bathroom with no bath or shower, also known as a powder room

Home Inspection One of the most important steps in the process of buying a home, the inspection is meant to identify any problems the house might have and to teach the customer about the home and how things work. The inspection will include the structure, basement, crawlspaces, appliances, interior and exterior, and electrical, heating and cooling, and plumbing systems.

Home Warranty a service contract that covers appliances and systems

Homeowner's Association a group of homeowners in any particular neighborhood or development who establish and enforce rules and maintain common property

Impervious not allowing entrance or passage. If siding is impervious to water, then water should not penetrate through the siding.

In Contract the moment when both buyer and seller sign a contract of sale

Inspection See Home Inspection

Interest the amount charged by a lending institution for the use of borrowed money

Interest-Only Mortgage a loan in which only the interest is paid on a monthly basis and the principal is owed in full at the end of the loan term

Landscape plants and trees on the outside of the property

Lender the person or company that lends the money to the buyer

Letter of Intent a formal statement that the buyer intends to purchase the property for a certain price on a certain date

Lien an encumbrance against the property

Liquidity investments or holdings that can be easily converted to cash

Listing(s) homes available for sale by real estate brokers

Loan Commitment a written statement that states which mortgage company has agreed to lend the buyer a certain amount of money at a certain interest rate for a specific period of time

Loan-to-Value Ratio the ratio of the amount of money you wish to borrow in comparison to the value of the home you wish to buy

Lock Box a box attached to the outside of a home to hold the house's key so other real estate professionals can gain access. A special key code is used to obtain entry. The box also records the comings and goings of all who enter.

Lot a portion of land; designated a "lot" for the purpose of identification

Maintenance monthly fees paid by condominium and co-operative owners as their share of the building's or complex's expenses

Mortgage a loan used to cover the cost of buying a home

Mortgage Points the points, or percentage of the total mortgage, the lender adds as an upfront cost for doing business

Multiple Listing Service (MLS) Available only to licensed real estate brokers and agents, MLS collects, compiles, and distributes information about homes listed for sale by its members

Offer the terms of purchase presented from a buyer to a seller. This can include the price, the closing period, and any contingencies such as repairs or the sale of the buyer's home.

Offer Accepted the moment when an owner accepts the offer from the buyer

Open House when a listing agent opens a house to the public for viewing

Open Kitchen a kitchen which opens up to the living space

Pass-Through Kitchen a kitchen with an opening from the kitchen into another room

Personal Property any movable property such as appliances, furniture, etc.

Pied à Terre an apartment maintained by someone who lives in another city

PITI Principal interest, taxes and insurance are the components of most mortgage payments

Points one percent of the total mortgage loan amount. Buyers often pay lenders a supplemental fee, calculated in points, to get a better interest rate on a particular mortgage

Possession the moment when the buyer can actually take possession of home

Powder Room See half-bath

Pre-approval an assessment of a potential borrower's ability to pay for a home, and a confirmation of the amount to be borrowed

Prime Rate an interest rate formally announced by a bank to be the lowest available at a particular time to its most credit-worthy customers. Borrowers considered to be low-risk receive loans at rates closer to prime than borrowers considered to be riskier.

Principal the amount of money borrowed. This does not include the interest paid to the lender.

Private Mortgage Insurance (PMI) insurance that protects the top 20 percent of a loan, often required for those who don't have a full 20 percent for a down payment

Radon a radioactive gas found in the ground or groundwater and formed by the decay of radium, usually found in small quantities in rock and soil

Ranch Style a modern style of home popularized in the 1950s and known for its one-story living

Real Estate Agent See Agent

Real Estate Broker a person, corporation, or partnership licensed to represent a buyer or seller in a real estate transaction. Brokers supervise licensed sales agents who then act for the broker.

Realtor a broker or agent who is a member of the National Association of Realtors

Reserve Fund a fund held by co-op directors to pay for future property expenses and upkeep

Row Houses See Townhouses

Sellers' broker represents sellers in real estate transactions. That broker's fiduciary responsibility is to negotiate the best possible price and terms for the seller. Any information shared by the seller with the seller's broker is to be kept confidential unless it is expressly indicated that the information can be shared.

Setback the distance from the front, back, and side of the lot in which construction can not occur without a variance

Superfund site any land identified by the Environmental Protection Agency (EPA) as a potential health or environmental risk and marked as a candidate for hazardous waste cleanup

Tax Deduction the amount a homeowner is allowed to subtract from the personal taxes he owes to the government

Tear-Down a house in such poor condition it is purchased primarily to be torn down so a new house can be built on the property

Time is of the essence A phrase used by attorneys defining a certain period of time in which an act must be performed

Title the right of ownership of a property

Title Insurance protection for both the lender and owner against unexpected or fraudulent claims of ownership

Townhouse Built in groups or rows, these are individual, private residences, in which one family occupies an entire building. Also known as Row Houses.

Variance a permit or license issued by the town to do something outside of usual building or zoning laws

Walk-Through the final inspection by the buyer before the closing

Walk-Through Kitchen a kitchen with two entrances and exits

Walk-Up Building a building without an elevator

Window Treatments curtains, blinds, or other treatments on a window

Real Estate Acronyms

4B/2B four bedrooms/two bathrooms

assum. fin. Assumable financing

dk deck

DR dining room

Dw dishwasher

gar garage

gard garden

EIK eat-in-kitchen

expansion pot'l potential for expansion

FDR formal dining room

FP fireplace

fplc fireplace

FR family room

frplc fireplace

grmet kit gourmet kitchen

HDW hardwood floors

Hdwd hardwood floors

HWF hardwood floors

hi ceils high ceilings

In-law pot'l potential for a separate apartment

lsd pkg leased parking area, may come with an additional cost

pvt private

pwdr rm powder room, or half-bath

upr upper floor

vu view

vw view

w/d washer/dryer

Internet Resources

American Society of Home Inspectors
www.Ashi.com

The Asbestos Institute
For more information on asbestos
www.asbestos-institute.ca/main.html

Bank Rate Monitor
Tips on interest rates and mortgage options
www.bankrate.com

Department of Housing and Urban Development (HUD)
Advice on homeownership and community development
www.hud.com

Environmental Protection Agency
Information on environmental concerns
www.epa.gov

Fannie Mae
National Mortgage Association
www.fanniemae.com

Federal Emergency Management Agency (FEMA)
Information on flood insurance and flood zones
www.fema.gov

Freddie Mac
Mortgage Information
www.freddiemac.com

National Association of Realtors
www.realtor.com

National Center for Home Equity Conversion
www.reverse.org

National Radon Safety Board
www.nrsb.org/nrsb-s1.htm

Real Estate.com
www.realestate.com

Your To-Do List during the Home Buying Process

While the process of buying a house varies by region across the country, many of the same steps need to occur from preparation through closing. The list below will give you insight into the steps that you'll routinely encounter during your home purchase, but always talk to your local real estate agent, attorney, title insurance company, and mortgage representative for the exact needs of your area and your transaction.

- Get a free copy of your credit report.
- Correct any errors on your credit report with your credit bureau and creditors.
- Examine your current monthly income and expenditures. Look for ways to save additional money.
- Determine how much you can afford for housing comfortably on a monthly basis.
- Contact a mortgage representative for available mortgage options and receive mortgage preapproval.
- Understand how real estate agencies work in your area.
- Find and select a real estate agent.
- Compare and select housing style: single family, condominium, or co-operative.
- Search for and find your "perfect" home.
- Review comparable property prices prior to making an offer.

- Review any available Sellers' Disclosure prior to making an offer.
- Offer and negotiate selling price, closing date, and any contingencies: home, pest, and radon inspections, mortgage and appraisal, deposit schedule, and selling of your current home.
- Have a local real estate attorney review the contract and contingencies.
- Complete the required mortgage paperwork for application.
- Schedule and attend the home inspection.
- Negotiate necessary home repairs.
- Research and arrange homeowners insurance.
- Research and arrange moving plans.
- Schedule the closing with an attorney or title insurance company as is appropriate for your area.
- Walk through the house on the day of the closing.
- Test all major systems.
- Look for any damage to property or appliances.
- Attend the closing where applicable.

Budget Plan

When you are trying to determine what you can comfortably afford in monthly mortgage payments, the best way to start is by looking at your current income and expenditures. Your tax preparer and financial planner will be excellent resources for advice regarding tax implications and budgeting concerns.

Determine your:

- current monthly loan payments: auto, student loan, personal loans
- fixed monthly expenses: childcare, gym memberships, cell phone plans
- variable monthly expenses: groceries, utilities, medical, and entertainment. Review your last twelve months' expenditures and develop a monthly average. Alternatively, keep a log of all expenses for two months and use the average of those two months.
- annual or semi-annual expenses: car insurance, health insurance, estimated federal or state taxes, payments to 401(k) or retirement plans
- income from traditional sources: full-time or part-time employment, investments, pensions
- income from less traditional sources: alimony, social security, payments from renters

Subtract the monthly average of your expenses from your monthly average income to determine the remainder.

Decide what portion of the remainder you want to earmark for saving and what portion should be allotted for unforeseen expenses such as emergency medical care, unplanned auto replacement, etc.

Share this income, expense, and planned savings information with your mortgage representative to determine the best mortgage level and mortgage vehicle for you.

Wish List and House Hunting Log

When determining what type of house you want to purchase, a wish list is a great place to start. Consider not only bedrooms, bathrooms, and price, but also important things like local utility providers and school districts. If you are buying a property with another person, both you and your partner should independently rank each feature you are looking for on a scale of one to five, with five being the most important. It is a great exercise in determining if the both of you are looking for the same amenities in a future home, and what is most important to you as a team and to you as an individual.

The following table can also be used as a log during your house hunting. As you walk through each house, note what features the dwelling has and doesn't have in comparison to your prioritized wish list. Keeping a log is a great way to remember the features of the many houses you see throughout the process.

Home Specifics	Ideal	Partner #1's priority ranking (1-5)	Partner #2's Priority ranking (1-5)	House #1: Address:	House #2: Address:
# of Bedrooms					
# of Baths					
Basement: finished, unfinished, partially finished, none					
Dining Room	Y/N				
Family Room	Y/N				
Kitchen: eat-in?	Y/N				
Home Office	Y/N				
Master Bedroom Suite	Y/N				
Garage	Y/N; size:				
Laundry Room	Y/N				
Deck, Patio					
Year built					
Home Style					
Condition: move-in, cosmetic repairs only, fixer-upper, knock-down					
Other:					

Exterior Features:				
Size of Yard				
Pool				
Privacy				
Neighborhood: quiet, active/busy, near shopping/school/transit				
School District				
Town				
Other:				
Finishing Details:				
Kitchen Counter Tops				
Kitchen Cabinets				
Kitchen Appliances Included: range, oven, refrigerator, microwave, water softener, dishwasher				
Flooring: carpet, hardwood, ceramic, vinyl				
Whirlpool Tub				
Vaulted Ceilings				

Moldings					
Other:					
Utility Preferences:					
Heat: oil, gas, propane, electric					
Cooking: oil, gas, propane, electric					
Cooling: fans, window a/c, central a/c					
Water: public or well					
Sewer: public, septic, cesspool					
Other:					
Financials:					
Price Range					
Taxes					
Maintenance Fees					
Additional Fees					
Other:					

Index

401(k), 125–126
5/25 mortgage, 104
7/23 mortgage, 104
80/10/10 loan, 103
80/15/5 loan, 103

A

adjustable–rate mortgage, 95–99, 105
ambient light, 228
amenities, 43, 160, 204, 242
amortization, 106
appraisal, 117, 119–120
APR, 86–87, 121
ARMs *see* adjustable rate mortgage
"as is"condition, 47, 221
asbestos, 282–285
assumable mortgage, 90
attorney review, 3, 262–267

B

balloon mortgage, 106–107
basement, 227–228, 235
bathroom, 13, 49, 172, 231
BC mortgage, 109–110, 118
biweekly mortgage, 102
budget, 35, 61, 64, 127, 130, 312–313
bungalow, 274
buyer's agent, 27–32

C

capital fee, 131

career, 8, 12–13, 34, 40, 116

CC&Rs, 181

Civil Rights Act of 1964, 56

Civil Rights Act of 1968, 56

closing, 219, 317, 321–337

colonial, 8

commission, 27–28, 31, 186, 250

commuting, 38, 41, 228

condominium ownership, 153–160

contingencies, 257–262

contract, 3, 86, 119, 167, 189, 192, 196, 212, 256–257, 259, 265, 267–268, 287–288, 335

contractor, 14, 138, 140, 147, 161, 169, 194, 271, 284–285, 287–288, 335

conventional mortgage, 89–90, 183–184

co-op board, 251–254

co-operative ownership, 153–160

counter offer, 248–249

countertops, 231

credit, 61–149

credit score, 65–69

    improvement of, 73–81

D

deck, 178, 301

deed, 55, 137–138, 154, 181, 198, 328–329

disclosure, 239, 251

discrimination, 57, 124

down payment, 100, 110

driveway, 136, 178

E

easement, 52, 176, 198, 239

easement appurtenant, 52

EIFS, 298–302

electromagnetic fields, 307

encroachment, 53

environmental concerns, 281–282

Equal Credit Opportunity Act, 120

escrow, 322-325

exclusions, 53–55

expansion, 174–182

Exterior Insulation Finish System *see* EIFS

F

Fair and Accurate Credit Transaction (FACT) Act, 74

Fair Housing Act, 56–57, 121

family room, 231

Fannie Mae, 88–90
Federal Housing Administration (FHA)
    FHA mortgage, 91, 101, 184
Federal Housing Finance Board, 16
Federal Truth-in-Lending laws, 86, 121
FEMA, 305
fence, 53, 179–180
feng shui, 235
FICO score, 65–68, 77, 79
fifteen-year loan, 92
fixed mortgage, 91–94
fixer-upper, 13
fixtures, 53
fizz-bo *see* for sale by owner
flood zones, 305–307
for sale by owner, 140, 185–196
Freddie Mac, 89–90
FSBO *see* for sale by owner

G

garage, 230, 233, 268
gifts (monetary) from family, 62–63
Ginnie Mae, 89
good faith estimate, 326

H

hardwood flooring, 232

historic status, 196–199

home equity loan, 183–184

Homeowners Association, 168–184

homeowners insurance, 141–142, 144, 149, 323

Homeowners Protection Act, 111

hot market, 10–11, 203

I

insect infestation, 273, 278–281

inspection, 3, 53, 221, 241, 251–261, 267–307, 318

insurance, 133, 136–149

interest rates, 113

interest-only loan, 97

internet, 22, 44, 62, 187, 199, 269–270, 292, 313

K

kitchen, 49, 172, 230

L

landmark status, 196–199

lead paint, 288–291

lending options, 62–63, 85–113

lien, 138

light fixtures, 54

loan, 61–149

lock-in, 113–114

M

maintenance, 9, 229

"Mansion Tax," 127

marriage, 9

mass transit, 39

master bedroom suite, 233

mechanic's lien, 138

"Millionaire's Tax," 127

mold, 291–293, 300

mortgage, 3, 8, 43, 61–149

mortgage representative, 64–65

Multiple Listing Service (MLS), 19

N

National Association of Home Builders (NAHB), 12

National Flood Insurance Program (NFIP), 305–306

National Register of Historic Places, 198

natural disasters, 145, 149

negative amortization, 98

negotiation, 20, 31, 46, 48, 115, 244–251, 255

neighborhood

   choice in, 1, 7, 34–45

new construction, 46, 48, 160–169

O

offer, 239–251, 254–262

oil tank, 224, 266, 302–304

open house, 21, 217, 219

overbuying, 16

P

PITI, 71

playroom, 15, 235

points, 114–115

pool, 177, 273

preapproval, 81–84

private mortgage insurance (PMI), 100, 110–113

purchase fee, 131

R

radon, 285–288

real estate agent

    bilingual, 25

    selecting, 3, 21–26

    costs, 3, 17

    working with, 16–21, 32–34

    vs. realtor, 17

    vs. broker, 18

real estate language and terms, 47–55

redlining, 124

Rehabilitation Act of 1973, 56

renovation, 169–185

rental, 8, 11, 63

repairs, 1, 194, 230, 311–314, 316–318

replacement insurance, 147

resale factors, 231–235

retirement, 93

rights of homeowners, 120–124

roof, 148, 170, 212, 227, 230, 270

S

schools, 41–43, 129, 208, 211, 213–222

second mortgage, 71

seller's agent, 27–32

sellers' market, 9

septic system, 224, 275–277

sewer, 224–225

shared appreciation mortgage, 107–108

square footage, 49, 50

steering, 57

sub-prime loan *see* BC mortgage

suburbs, 1, 162

sunroom, 15

survey, 46, 53, 136, 176, 239

T

tax, 124–132, 188, 197, 322, 323

tax lien, 138, 322–323

termites, 279–280, 299–300

thirty-year loan, 88, 92, 94

title, 130, 137, 146, 324–326, 328, 335

title insurance, 136–149

townhouse, 155

trash removal, 224

travel, 37, 40–41

two-step mortgage, 105

U

underbuying, 16
utilities, 225–226

V

VA loan, 105–106

W

walk-in closet, 233
walkout basement, 235
walk-through, 314–318
wallpaper, 234
warranty, 133–135
water damage, 142, 316
wells, 266, 294–298
wish list, 13–16

Z

zoning, 55, 174–176, 178–179

About
the
Author

As a licensed realtor, Michael Flynn specializes in helping both residential sellers and buyers from entry-level condominiums and starter homes to million-dollar-plus properties. Prior to his career in real estate, Michael worked for two marketing agencies—whose clients included Fortune 500 companies—and gained experience that has been extremely useful in marketing and selling real estate.

Michael works for Weichert Realtors, in the Basking Ridge, NJ office, and works with buyers and sellers in Union, Morris, and Somerset counties.

Professional Affiliations

- Member of National Association of Realtors
- Member of NJ Association of Realtors
- Member of North Central Jersey Board of Realtors
- Member of Garden State Multiple Listing Service

For more information about Michael, go to www.weichert.com or www.realtor.com.

Notes:

_____

_____

_____

_____

_____

_____

_____

_____

_____

_____

_____

_____

_____

_____

_____

_____

_____

_____

_____

_____

_____

Notes:

Notes: